# CATS'
# TALES

# CATS' TALES

## Gyles Brandreth

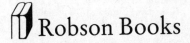 Robson Books

Cartoons by Mike Buckner
Designed by Harold King

First published in Great Britain in 1986 by Robson Books Ltd.,
Bolsover House, 5-6 Clipstone Street, London W1P 7EB.

Copyright © 1986 Gyles Brandreth

**British Library Cataloguing in Publication Data**

Brandreth, Gyles
   Cats' tales.
   1. Cats——Anecdotes, facetiae, satire, etc.
   I. Title
   636.8'00207     SF445.5

   ISBN 0-86051-406-4

Typeset by Bookworm Typesetting, Manchester
Printed in Great Britain by Whitstable Litho Ltd., Whitstable.
Bound by WBC Bookbinders Ltd., Maesteg.

**In memory of
ROSIE
(1974–1984)**

# CONTENTS

# Acknowledgements

I must thank Oscar, Neville and Rosie who have taught me so much; and Sandy Ransford and Gillian Denton, who have marshalled the research material with such zeal, good humour and distinction.

My thanks also to Francis Loney, David Smith, Leonard Hodge, Martin Davison, Francesca Findlater and the staff at the RSPCA. I am grateful to Faber and Faber for permission to reproduce T.S. Eliot's 'The Naming of Cats' from *Old Possum's Book of Practical Cats*, and to Express Newspapers for permission to reproduce King Cat from the *Star*.

My special thanks to my colleagues at TV-am who helped organize the Feline Personality of the Year Award, notably Alison Field who handled the thousands of entries.

And last, but by no means least, for without them there would have been no competition, my thanks to all the entrants who so painstakingly logged their cats' achievements and foibles, and particularly to the following, who supplied extra photographs for this book: Ruth Keridge, Cathie Varley, the Bishton family, Nicola Summers, Edith Mitchell, Muriel Lee and R.D. Stewart.

# INTRODUCTION

**Cat.** A well-known carnivorous quadruped which has long been domesticated, being kept to destroy mice, and as a house pet.

The *Oxford English Dictionary*'s definition is all very well as far as it goes, but it doesn't go very far, does it? A cat is utterly indefinable, of course, but there's still a lot more to it than that. In my book the definition would be rather more comprehensive:

> **Cat.** A well-known, much-loved, universally respected, occasionally misunderstood carnivorous quadruped (that also eats cereal and cheese and goodness knows what else and sometimes walks on two legs not four) which has long been domesticated, being kept to destroy mice, curtain linings, table legs, etc., and as a house pet, inimitable conversationalist, boon companion and matchless four-legged friend.

The joy of cats lies in their infinite variety. They come in all shapes and sizes and their personalities are as various as their appearances. Extrovert, introvert, athletic, lazy, serene, soppy, independent, devoted – there's a cat to match every adjective you can think of, even the ones, let's face it, that characterize the negative rather than the positive traits of the feline personality. Most cats, of course, are loving, giving, gorgeous and fun, but in the history of the world there have been one or two (well, three or four; very well, a dozen – *at most*) who haven't been all that they might be. However, if you know a cat that's aloof and unloving, don't blame the cat, blame the human it lives with. If anything's wrong (I was going to say 'not up to scratch') with a cat of your acquaintance, the fault lies in the nurture not the nature. Cats are fundamentally *perfect*. That's what I think anyway.

I am biased, of course. Cats have been part and parcel of my life since birth. Griggs, the cat of my childhood, would follow me to school. He was essentially a London cat, knew the *A to Z* like the back of his paw. (He got hopelessly lost in Glasgow, though. It was New Year's Eve, not a night for a cat to be out on the loose in the Gorbals in the 1950s. Foolishly we let him out of the car for a five-minute amble and five hours later we were roaming the streets calling 'Griggs! Griggsy! Where are you, puss?' while revelling Scots reeled about us. Eventually, we abandoned the search and collapsed, miserable and exhausted, into our beds at the hotel. After breakfast we returned to the car and found Griggs perched complacently on the bonnet. I'll swear he was humming 'Auld Lang Syne'.)

Currently there are two priceless pussy-cats in the Brandreth household. They are a pair from a set of triplets we acquired from a Greek restaurant in Baker Street twelve years ago. I can't say that we saved them from becoming kebabs because it's an excellent restaurant and they would have been reared there beautifully, but when we saw them, only a day or two after their births, we were seduced instantly and asked if we could adopt them. The largest we named Oscar (because he looked wild!); we thought his sister was his brother and because to me he looked wilder I wanted to call him Thornton, but my wife said he looked exactly like a chap she knew called Neville so that's what he's called – only he isn't a he, he's a she, except that truth be told she's really an it these days. (I know Mrs Gillick wouldn't approve, but we introduced compulsory contraception among our kittens at a relatively tender age.) The third member of the tribe was Rosie, who died of throat cancer two years ago. She is much missed.

At home, as well as the two cats of our own, we have photographs of at least two thousand others. We have all these wonderful feline photos simply because at the beginning of 1986 on TV-am I launched a nationwide search for Britain's Feline Personality of the Year. I was looking for the country's most charismatic cat – a moggie with the most, a pussy with pizzazz, a kitty with class – and I found hundreds and thousands. From all over the United Kingdom (and from Adelaide, Abu Dhabi

and Wisconsin!) proud cat-owners submitted pictures and written evidence testifying to the unique nature and unrivalled charismatic quality of their own personal pussy-cats.

I thought it would be nice to have a verbal and pictorial account of some of the most remarkable cats in Britain today and that's what *Cats' Tales* is. It is a little more than that too, because as well as pictures and stories of some unusually attractive (and attractively unusual) cats I have included a range of other cat-orientated elements – from some sound advice on cat care (from experts) to invaluable tips on how to take photographs of your pets (from *the* expert), from the best and worst cat jokes I know (I admit they're dreadful but I can't resist them) to the most intriguing facts and figures about cats of all kinds that have come my way. I hope you enjoy the book and that your cat does too. (Cats *love* being read aloud to. Didn't you know?)

# VICTORIAN VALUES

The Royal Society for the Prevention of Cruelty to Animals was founded in 1824. Queen Victoria took a great interest in it, and ordered that a medal, known as the Queen's Medal, should be prepared for presentation to the Society's most notable workers. A design was created and submitted to the Queen, who noticed that there was no cat among the animals depicted and directed that a cat should be placed in the foreground of the medal – she even sketched one in on the design. She said she felt it was time that the Royal Family tried to change the general feeling of aversion to and contempt for cats that then prevailed, and later wrote to the Society, specifically requesting that they should do something for the protection and safety of cats, which were generally misunderstood and badly ill-treated.

# HAUNTING TAILS

Humans are not the only beings to haunt the living when they themselves are dead. Cats, too, have been known to make spectral appearances, though often, it is claimed, they are felt rather than seen. People have reported phantom cats jumping onto their beds, or rubbing against their legs. On at least two occasions, in recent years, however, they have actually put in an appearance.

In a restaurant in Battle, Sussex, the ghost of a medium-sized black cat has been seen on an upstairs landing by three previous owners and their families and friends. It generally glides along a corridor and then vanishes when it reaches a particular bedroom door, although on two occasions it sat at the top of the stairs for a while before vanishing.

And a house in Wimbledon, South-West London, is haunted by half a black and white cat! That is, only its rear end has ever been seen, at the corner of a bedroom wall, as if it were about to walk round into the corridor. The owner has a pet black cat which lives in the house and which appears to be puzzled, rather than frightened, by the ghost's appearance.

# GENE MACHINE

There is an old joke which asks how one tells the sex of a chromosome, the reply being to take its genes off, for, as we all know, a gene is the part of a cell which carries the blueprint for the reproduction of hereditary characteristics.

In the cat-breeding world, people talk of certain colours being dominant and certain colours being recessive, an example being the blue of the Siamese's eyes, which never appears in a cross-bred cat. The original colour of the cat is thought to be the striped tabby, which is the colour nearest to that of a wild cat. But now scientists have discovered that the blotched tabby is taking over the cat world. The blotched tabby gene, which is a dominant one, is carried by more than 80 per cent of British cats and by more than 60 per cent of French cats, so in the future it could be that most of the moggies seen around Britain will have the blotched tabby colouring.

However, this dominant colouring does not seem to have reached the Scottish islands, which contain cats distinctly different from those on the mainland. There are many marmalade and tortoiseshell cats, due, it is believed, to the original Viking settlers taking cats with those colourings to the islands. And the island of Yell, in the Shetlands, is distinguished by having the highest-known frequency in the world of white cats.

Oliver, aged eight weeks, winner of the Cutest Kitten of the Year Award. He is owned by the Bishton family of Rottingdean, East Sussex.

# THE SUN RISES ON NEKOGO

For hundreds of years legends and superstitions concerning cats have abounded in Japan, where they were only kept to keep down vermin. It is only in the last thirty years or so that they have been kept as pets, and suddenly, in the 1980s, they have become immensely popular. Fortunately for the cat, it is now considered necessary to feed it rather than leave it to catch mice, and pet supplies counters have sprung up in department stores, and large quantities of books and magazines on cats and cat care are now on sale.

The most famous Japanese legend about cats concerns the Lord of Nabeshima who lived hundreds of years ago on the island of Kyushu. He hated cats, especially after his favourite, Otoyo, was killed by a monster cat which afterwards assumed the spirit of the dead Otoyo and returned each night to work magic against the Lord of Nabeshima. The lord's servants sat up all night praying to protect their master from this evil magic, and the monster cat was so impressed by their loyalty that she stopped her magic. From this story the cat passed into Japanese legend as a wise friend to all who are kind to cats and an evil enemy to those who hate them.

The Japanese language is full of allusions to cats. People with round faces are called *Nekozura* (a face like a cat), people with soft persuasive voices are called *Nekonadegoe* (a voice like a cat). The Japanese for kitten, or pussy, is *Nekogo*, and there are proverbs in Japanese about cats, such as *Neko ni koban* (giving a gold coin to a cat, i.e. giving something that is worthless to its recipient) and *Neko ni katsubishi* (showing dried fish to a cat, or offering an irresistible temptation). There is even a bridge in Tokyo called *Nekomata-bashi*, after a cat which tried to relieve its mistress's poverty by stealing gold from a local money-lender!

The Japanese believe that cats have souls, so there can be a religious service for a dead cat, and ceremonies are held at Oizumi cemetary in Tokyo for the souls of departed felines. Cats appear frequently in Japanese art, too – often accompanied by *matanabe*, a red- and white-leaved vine which cats love and which is sold in powdered form as a cats' medicine. Cat toys and models are very popular. Japanese babies get 'lucky' felt cats at their naming ceremonies, and on 3 March each year, when the Japanese hold doll festivals all over the country, one of the most popular types features a figure riding on a cat. However, despite all this adoration, the traditional covering for Japanese musical instruments is *Neko-no-kawa* – cat skin – and it is only in recent years that people have started campaigning to stop its use.

# ROOM 8 – THE CLASSROOM CAT

Room 8 was an American tabby and white tom cat who one day in 1953 turned up at Elysian Heights Elementary School in Baxter Street, Los Angeles. He wandered round the classrooms, enjoying titbits from the children's lunches, and for some reason seemed to have a preference for Room 8 – hence his name.

He turned up faithfully for lessons every day, even when it was pouring down with rain. In the evenings, and in school holidays, he vanished, and no one knew where he went.

The cat became the school mascot, loved by pupils and staff alike for his kindly nature. He never minded being fussed over by the children, but seemed to enjoy the attention, and as time went on he became widely known as a character. He appeared several times on television, and a book was written about him. Royalties from the book about Room 8 and gifts of money enclosed in fan mail were used to boost the school's library fund. He attended Elysian Heights for fifteen years, and during this time received more than 10,000 letters, mostly from children but some purporting to be from other cats. They were dutifully answered by sixth-grade students who signed them all with a special paw-print stamp.

In later years Room 8 was looked after in the school holidays by a family who lived near the school and whose four children

attended it, but he was fed at school in term time by specially appointed 'feeders' among the pupils.

Sadly all good things come to an end, and the cat who had seen children all through their schooldays died in 1968, aged approximately twenty-two, of kidney failure. Because of his great popularity a Room 8 fund was established after his death and used to maintain a children's bed at a Los Angeles orthopaedic hospital. Gifts of books, magazine subscriptions and so on are still sent to the school in Room 8's name, to the benefit of the pupils now there. It is a fitting memorial to this dearly loved cat that his memory should be kept alive by gifts which benefit children after his death.

# CAT-ANATOMY

The cat is a wonder of nature, perfectly equipped for the life it is intended to lead. It is amazingly agile, very strong and muscular for its small size, and able to move slowly, stealthily and almost silently, or with surprising speed over a short distance. But it cannot sustain this and needs to rest between bursts of violent activity.

A cat in its natural state is a hunter, often active by night. Its eyes are specially adapted for this, being able to dilate enormously to allow it to see in very dim light. Conversely the pupils can also contract to narrow slits to protect the eye from very bright light. The cat's third eyelid, a membrane which is normally invisible but which can sometimes be seen in the corner of the eye when it is unwell, can also be raised to protect the eye. Because the eyes both face forwards, as in a human, the cat has stereoscopic vision, which makes it a good judge of distances. Animals whose eyes are set on opposite sides of their head see two images which makes them poor judges of distance.

Compared with a human a cat has a highly sensitive sensory system. Its hearing is acute, which is one reason why it is so upset by loud noises and people shouting, and it has a highly developed sense of smell. Many cats will sniff delicately round their owners' feet and clothing when they return to the house, discovering, through the sense of smell, what the owner has been doing and where he or she has been. The cat's whiskers and long 'eyebrow' hairs, known as the vibrissae, are also highly sensitive, this time to touch, and help it feel its way and detect the presence of objects.

Cats are superb acrobats. The old adage 'a cat always lands on its feet' is largely true, and special sequences of photographs have shown how a cat twists its body round when falling to enable it to land feet first. It is not, however, capable of surviving falls from a height any more than any other animal is. The thoracic (chest area) spine of the cat has more flexibility than that of most other mammals, including humans, which is why it can bend over and wash in the extraordinarily contorted positions many cats adopt. The tail acts as a balancing agent, helping the cat to walk along narrow ledges that would be impossible for most animals.

A cat has five claws on the forepaws and four on the hind. The claws have a special retracting mechanism enabling the animal to flash them out in defence or attack, or to sheathe them to allow it to walk silently or to show affection to its friends. The stropping of claws that causes so much distress to some cat owners is to keep them clean and ready for action, helping to remove dead layers of 'nail', which can often be found lying beneath favourite stropping areas. The claws are invaluable in climbing, catching prey and, of course, fighting, where the less sharp but immensely strong hind claws are often used to rake an opponent if the cat is on its back.

Teeth, too, are specially designed for catching, killing and eating prey. The long, curved canines kill the prey and tear it, the pointed molars and pre-molars slice the flesh into pieces small enough to swallow, and the tiny incisors help remove flesh from bones. The rough surface of the tongue helps in this action, too, as well as being a useful grooming tool.

Scent glands on the cat's forehead, lips, chin and tail are used to leave scent messages on anything a cat rubs up against, including its owner! It is probably marking you out as its property against the claims of other cats. A sensitive human nose can sometimes detect a cat's scent (which has nothing to do with the unpleasant tom-cat smell) on its forehead. Siamese, in particular, have a very pleasant scent.

# SIAMESE, IF YOU PLEASE

With its vivid blue eyes, distinctive colouring and unique voice, the Siamese is probably the one pedigree cat that everyone recognises. In cat breeders' language Siamese belong to the Foreign Short-hair type, all of which are distinguished by their long, lean bodies, wedge-shaped heads with large ears, long tails, oval feet and short, sleek coats.

Siamese cats with seal-point colouring were known in Thailand 400 years ago, and it is believed that they first became noticed by Europeans in the 1790s. But it was nearly a hundred years later that they were brought to Europe. In their native country they had been the special pets of the court, rather than the kind of cat you see in the street, and when the first representatives of the breed came to the West they were presents from the Thai royal family and were known as the Royal Cats of Siam. After this first introduction the breed quickly became established in the West, and the Siamese Cat Society of America was founded in 1909.

In the early days of the breed the cats were more heavily built than they are today, and they often had a kink in their tails and cross eyes. The modern Siamese should have a long body, slim legs and small, oval-shaped feet. The head should narrow to a small muzzle, with a straight profile, large pointed ears and almond-shaped eyes that slope upwards and outwards. The coat should be short, of fine texture and lying close to the body.

There are several different kinds of Siamese colouring but all have a pale body with mask and points of darker fur, extending over the feet and lower legs, the tail and the ears. A seal-point has a cream body colour with dark brown points; a chocolate-point has points of a lighter brown and an ivory-coloured coat; a blue-point is white, with blue-grey points; a lilac-point is a milky colour with pinkish-grey points; a red-point has a white coat with reddish-gold points. In addition there are cream-points, in which the points are not much darker than the body colour; tortie-points, with tortoiseshell points, and tabby-points, with tabby striped ones.

From the Siamese have been bred the Burmese, the Foreign White, the Foreign Black and the Havana.

Apart from its colouring the most distinctive characteristic of the Siamese is its voice – a yowling noise which has been compared to the cry of a baby. They produce a wide range of sounds and often seem to 'talk', both to themselves and to their owners, much to the astonishment of their non-aficionados. They tend to be very affectionate cats, happy to be with their owners even if moved around from place to place. They are extremely intelligent too, and owners sometimes tire of having to devise means of thwarting them! They can be very wilful – even more so than most cats – and sometimes spiteful when crossed, and are likely to be very sorry for themselves when ill. Because they have such strong characters people either love them or loathe them. What kind of cat person are you?

# CAT
# VENERATION

The domestic cat is thought to have originated in Ancient Egypt, and enormous numbers of monumental drawings of cats have survived from there. Also, many mummified bodies of cats have been found by archaeologists – cats were, by law, honoured in death even by ordinary people, and the Pharaoh Thotmes IV built a temple dedicated to his cats.

But the most powerful cat of all was the cat-headed goddess Pasht or Bast. She was goddess of the moon, hunting and love, and was both good and evil. She was thought to be most powerful at a time of solar eclipse when she fought, and of course always beat, the powers of darkness in battle for light for the world. In Egyptian law, killing a cat was a crime punishable by death.

The Greeks did not have much knowledge of the domestic cat, but the Romans did, and revered them. The Roman goddess of Liberty was portrayed with a cup in one hand, a sceptre in the other and a cat at her feet.

The prophet Muhammad loved cats, and is supposed to have cut off his sleeve rather than disturb his beloved cat Muezza who was asleep on it. Even today, cats, but not dogs, are allowed in mosques. Hindus, too, worshipped cats, and all the faithful were expected to open their houses to them.

Cat-worship spread throughout Europe until, in the fifteenth century, Pope Innocent VIII ordered cat-worshippers to be burned as witches. For many hundreds of years after this, cats were connected with witchcraft and were thought to be a witch's most valuable familiar. As a result they were often terribly persecuted. Not until the late eighteenth century did cats come into their own again, first as prized mousers and finally as beloved pets.

# GETTING A KITTEN

Before you acquire a kitten, do consider carefully if you are going to have the time, space and energy to look after it properly every day for the whole of its life – sixteen years or so if you are lucky. *Don't* buy one on the spur of the moment, or as a present for someone. Consider your surroundings. If you live on or near a busy road it is not a good idea to have a cat, as most cats have little road sense. If you live in a flat, without access to a garden or open space, cat-ownership is not a good idea either, as cats like fresh air and sunshine just as we do, and need grass to eat (see page 51).

If you do decide to get a kitten, it is best to choose a reputable source, such as a breeder, someone known to you, a vet or animal welfare society, rather than a pet shop. Kittens often go to pet shops far too young, and they are often not very healthy as a result.

A kitten should not be taken away from its mother until it is at least eight weeks old. It will need to be transported in a pet-carrying box or basket, and before you take it home you should have decided where it will sleep, and which areas of the house (if any) you are going to ban it from. You should arrange a bed for it and its own feeding dishes which should always be placed in the same spot. It will need a litter tray, too, which again should always be kept in the same place. The point about making all these little rules is that if the young animal knows what it is allowed to do and where it is allowed to go, and if the rules never vary, then it will grow up to be well-behaved and with a sense of security. If one member of the household allows it to jump on the kitchen table and another shoos it off then it will be confused and unhappy.

A cardboard box with one of the sides cut down makes a good bed, and you should line it with something soft and warm to sleep on and raise it off the floor out of draughts. For the first few nights a warm (not hot) hot-water bottle wrapped in a blanket or an old sweater will be appreciated.

Kittens love to explore, so be sure that any dangers are locked out of harm's way. Any taboo places (such as the top of the cooker) must be kept out of bounds with a firm 'No'. Kittens also tire quickly, and should be allowed to sleep undisturbed when they wish to do so. Young children especially must be discouraged from constantly disturbing the kitten, and must be taught not to shout and scream at it, as cats are frightened of loud noises.

Find out from the previous owner what kind of foods the kitten has been used to and avoid any radical changes in diet. It should be fed along the lines suggested on page 50, with the addition of milk and cereal, but will need four small meals a day from the age of eight weeks to fourteen weeks, and three small meals a day from fourteen weeks to six months. After that it can be fed as an adult cat.

By the time a kitten is eight weeks old it will have been toilet-trained by its mother to a certain extent, but you need to be on hand for a few days to reinforce this training. When you first bring the kitten home, show it its litter tray, and scrape its paws gently in it. As soon as it wakes from a sleep, or has eaten a meal, guide it to the tray, and when it has performed, stroke it and tell it it is a good cat. Cats are naturally clean and soon get the idea. In order to encourage it to use the tray, make sure the tray is kept clean, as no cat likes to have to tread in its own dirt. If the kitten makes a mistake and performs elsewhere, say 'No' firmly and carry it to its tray and make encouraging sounds. Never shout at it or hit it or 'rub its nose in it' – the kitten will be frightened and confused and will not understand why you are being nasty. Clean the area with disinfectant and the smell will discourage it from using the same place again.

Of course, you probably hope that your cat will use the garden for toilet purposes, but a kitten should not be allowed outside until it has been vaccinated against feline infectious enteritis and cat flu. These vaccinations are normally given at ten weeks and thirteen weeks.

Unless you have a pedigree kitten and are sure you want to breed from it, it is best to have it neutered, whether it is male or female. Apart from the problem of bringing more unwanted kittens into the world (the RSPCA destroyed 61,743 unwanted cats and kittens in 1985 and 66,523 in 1984), tom cats are likely to roam and get involved in road accidents, to fight and get injured, and they also have the unpleasant habit of spraying evil-smelling urine about the place. Your veterinary surgeon will advise you on the best age to neuter a kitten, but it is at approximately three to four months for females and between three and six months for males. The kitten will soon recover from the operation, and will be a more contented and home-loving cat than its un-neutered counterpart.

This is nine-week-old Cassie, winner of the Show Stopping Look of the Year. Cassie is owned by nine-year-old Nicola Summers of Heswall on Merseyside. He is a good cat who does most things a dog can do except bark, and this wonderful pose, which won him the award, was the result of telling him to 'think of Gyles Brandreth'!

# GREATEST NUMBER OF KITTENS

Cats usually give birth to between one and nine kittens, depending upon the age and breed of the mother. The largest instant family ever recorded was that born to a Burmese called Tara in 1970. Her five minutes' indiscretion with a half-Siamese Casanova in a barn resulted in nineteen offspring, of which, amazingly, fifteen were hale and hearty.

Another mother to produce a larger litter was a Canadian Siamese called Tikatoo. She produced fifteen kittens in 1976, all of which survived.

Un-neutered female cats produce two or three litters a year when in their prime. Dusty, a tabby, of Bonham, Texas, USA, obviously enjoyed motherhood. She produced 420 kittens during her breeding life. Another tabby, Tippy, of Kingston-upon-Hull, Humberside, holds the British record, producing her 343rd kitten in 1933 when aged twenty-one.

# THE KITTEN AND FALLING LEAVES

See the kitten on the wall
Sporting with the leaves that fall,
Withered leaves—one—two—and three –
From the lofty elder tree!

– But the kitten, how she starts,
Crouches, stretches, paws, and darts!
First at one, and then its fellow
Just as light and just as yellow;
There are many now – now one -
Now they stop and there are none.
What intenseness of desire
In her upward eye of fire!
With a tiger-leap half way
Now she meets the coming prey,
Lets it go as fast, and then
Has it in her power again:
Now she works with three or four,
Like an Indian conjurer,
Quick as he in feats of art,
Far beyond in joy of heart . . .

WILLIAM WORDSWORTH (1770–1850)

★★★★★★★★★★★★★★★★★★★★★★★★★★★★★★★★★★★★★

Pusskins, winner of the Feline Personality of the Year
Award. Pusskins has lived with Mrs Ruth Kerridge of
Havant, Hampshire, since he turned up on her doorstep as
a stray five years ago. He is an adventurous cat who climbs
trees and fences and explores all the neighbours' gardens.
He is alert, discerning and independent, with a sense of
humour and an optimistic spirit, and when he wants
something, he sits up and begs, pawing the air with his
front paws. You may wonder what is so unusual about all
these things in a cat. Well, Pusskins is quite blind, and it is
because of his tremendous spirit and courage in adversity,
as well as his great personality, that he won the award.

★★★★★★★★★★★★★★★★★★★★★★★★★★★★★★★★★★★★★

# TOM, DICK OR HARRY?

Unlike humans, cats may produce a number of young at one time, which have been fathered by several different mates. In fact, it is not impossible for every kitten in a litter to have a different father, since it is the sexual act itself which triggers off the release of an egg, and a female cat may be served by a number of males in quick succession.

Indeed, a black and white female of ill repute gave birth to a litter consisting of one black and white Manx, one tabby and white Manx, one tabby and white tailed, one tortoiseshell and white tailed, and one perfect seal-pointed Siamese. Well, variety is the spice of life!

# MOST POPULAR CAT BREEDS

The most popular (i.e. the most commonly found) type of cat in the world is, of course, the ordinary, cross-bred moggie. There are millions of such cats in every country in the world, and millions of owners who feel privileged to be allowed to provide for their common moggie.

But among the pedigree cats, far and away the most popular is the Siamese, with Tortoiseshells, Abyssinians, Burmese and various kinds of long-hairs (Persians) the runners-up.

# SHOWING OFF

The first proper cat show was held in London in 1871 at the Crystal Palace. There were 170 entries, but it was not until 1887 that the various societies involved in setting up the show got together to form the National Cat Club. The National Cat Club organized a stud book and register of pedigree cats, and later developed into the single British organization controlling breed societies and cat clubs, the Governing Council of the Cat Fancy. Breed standards are strictly controlled by the council, and they make decisions as to whether or not a new breed should be accorded recognition, and so on.

The Governing Council holds a Supreme Show in May each year at the National Exhibition Centre in Birmingham. Only cats that have won at local shows qualify for entry, so in effect all the entrants are champions!

The other major cat show in Britain, and one with which the general public may be more familiar, is the National Cat Club Show which is held in the autumn of each year at Olympia in London. Any cat can enter this show – even a non-pedigree one – for there are special classes for pet cats along with those for specific breeds.

# FANS AND FOES

Cat lovers are to be found in many different walks of life. Louis Pasteur, Albert Einstein and Albert Schweitzer were all devoted to cats, as was Sir Isaac Newton, who owned two which presided over his barn. He is credited not only with propounding gravitational laws, but also, more importantly, with inventing the cat-flap.

Many monarchs, too, have favoured cats. Frederick the Great of Prussia, Louis XV of France and Queen Victoria were all great cat lovers. But there is no cat resident in Buckingham Palace now; corgi usurpers hold sway.

The Church has long had ailurophiles at its helm. Pope Leo XII was so besotted with his cat, Micetto, that he used to give audiences with the cat hidden in his sleeve. Cardinal Richelieu, too, was devoted to cats and used to choose twelve favoured ones to share his bed at night. Cardinal Wolsey also kept a cat, present at all his cathedral services. The present Pontiff is reputed to love all animals, so it is fairly safe to say that the Vatican is some hallowed moggie's home.

Cats and dictators, for some reason, don't seem to have got on at all well. Napoleon loathed them, as did Genghis Khan, Julius Caesar and Mussolini. Hitler may have been the exception who proves the rule.

# THE CAT WHO COUNTERED A KING

This story is some 450 years old so there is no way of knowing how much of it is true. It has passed down to us as legend, but most legends have some basis in fact. But whatever its provenance, it is a charming tale, which is why it is included in this book.

When Henry VIII became King of England a nobleman called Sir Henry Wyatt held the position of Keeper of the Jewels, a function he had also performed for Henry VII. Sir Henry was a highly respected man, a friend of Sir Thomas More, the Lord Chancellor – and, so the story goes, a cat lover. He was accompanied by his cat everywhere he went, and when the Court moved to a different palace, the cat went too.

In due course, like many other noblemen, Sir Henry Wyatt fell foul of Henry VIII and was imprisoned in the Tower of London, locked away in a cold, damp dungeon without any food. He would quickly have starved to death, which was presumably the King's intention, had it not been for his cat. The cat used to slip out through the bars of the cell each day and return bearing its master a pigeon, which the jailer, out of pity, used to cook for him to eat. Sir Henry lived for some time on the victims of his cat's hunting, and eventually, since he did not die, was released, having been kept alive by the cat who thwarted the wishes of one of the most powerful of English monarchs.

# TO A CAT

Cat! who has pass'd thy grand climacteric,
   How many mice and rats hast in thy days
   Destroy'd? – How many tit bits stolen? Gaze
With those bright languid segments green, and prick
Those velvet ears – but pr'ythee do not stick
   Thy latent talons in me – and upraise
   Thy gentle mew – and tell me all thy frays
Of fish and mice, and rats and tender chick.
Nay, look not down, nor lick thy dainty wrists -
   For all the wheezy asthma, – and for all
Thy tail's tip is nick'd off – and though the fists
   Of many a maid have given thee many a maul,
Still is that fur as soft as when the lists
   In youth thou enter'dst on glass bottled wall.

JOHN KEATS (1795–1821)

'*But I* don't *encourage them – I just give them something to eat*'

Susie, aged twenty-nine, winner of the Oldest Cat in the Kingdom Award. Susie is a neutered male cat who was fortunate enough to be taken in by Mrs Edith Mitchell in 1957 when he was very young. He had been shot by an air pistol and lost an eye as a result. His first twenty-one years were spent in the Lavender Hill area of London, where he was one of the 'mob'! His owner says he has always been a happy and contented cat, but sadly in 1985 he was savaged by a dog, resulting in a dislocated hip and deafness. He now lives in South Harrow, Middlesex, and, despite his injuries and lack of teeth due to his advanced years, he still manages to get about and grows more affectionate the older he gets.

# LONGEST-LIVED CATS

Cats live longer than any other small domestic animals. Ages of fifteen to seventeen are not at all unusual, and quite a number of cats living beyond thirty have been reported. Ma, a female tabby which lived in Devon, holds the record for longevity, dying in 1957 aged thirty-four years and five months. Bobby of Wexford in Eire, and Selina of Wellingborough, Northamptonshire, both made it to thirty-two.

# CATS CONSCRIPTION

Cats have often been unwilling victims of scientific research. The pros and cons of this are endlessly debatable, but it is certain that man has not hesitated to use them for any purpose.

Once or twice, however, the tables have been turned, and a few experiments have gone somewhat awry.

During the recent Vietnam war, the US army decided that because of their ability to see clearly even in near pitch-darkness, cats would be invaluable guides for soldiers on night patrol in the jungle. Accordingly, in 1968, a 'platoon' of highly-trained guide cats were shipped out to Vietnam. Here is a summing up of the final army report on the mission:

> A squad, upon being ordered to move out, was led off in all different directions by the cats; on many occasions the animals led their troops racing through thick bush in pursuit of field mice . . . often the animals would stalk and attack [wait for it] the dangling pack straps of the soldier immediately in front of them. If the weather was inclement, or even threatening inclemency, the cats were never anywhere to be found.

# FEEDING TIME

A cat's natural diet is raw meat from prey it has killed, but since it consumes the whole of that prey it takes in more than just meat – for example, vegetable matter from the creature's stomach, its fur or feathers, bones, and so on. Therefore we have to try and feed a balanced diet to our cats, and while this should be based on raw or cooked meat they will benefit from the addition of offal – heart, liver and kidneys – from time to time; cereals, in the form of brown bread or cooked rice, and a small amount of vegetable matter, such as cooked cabbage, sprouts, beans, carrots, and so on. Cooked fish can be substituted for meat occasionally.

Reputable brands of tinned foods provide a balanced diet and are a convenient way of feeding a cat, but you should try and feed fresh foods some of the time. After all, you wouldn't like to live on tinned foods, would you?

The more varied your cat's diet the less likely it is to suffer from dietary deficiences, but if it seems listless or has a poor coat, is recovering from an illness, or is a pregnant or nursing mother, it will benefit from brewer's yeast, easily obtained in tablet form. Small amounts of cod or halibut liver oil will be beneficial, too.

Cats should not be overfed. The general rule for feeding a healthy, adult cat with access to a garden for exercise is 4oz (100g) of food per 10lb (5kg) of body weight per day. If the cat lives indoors and cannot exercise much then these amounts should be reduced. On the other hand, a mother cat could need between 8oz (225g) and 1lb (450g) of extra food per day.

Cats will also appreciate scraps from the table – bits of meat, gravy, roast chicken skin, etc., but should not be fed on these exclusively, nor should they be fed as titbits between meals.

An adult cat should be fed once or twice a day though an old cat will do better with two or three smaller meals rather than one large one. If feeding once only, then make sure this is at night so you can get the cat in. Try and feed your cat at regular hours – all living creatures thrive on routine – and always feed him or her in the same place. Make sure there is a bowl of clean, fresh water by the food bowl at all times, even though your cat may not seem to drink very much. Make sure the bowls are kept clean and rinsed free of detergent, and never clean them with a carbolic preparation as this is dangerous to cats. Although dry foods are convenient, don't feed them too often. Cats can get dehydrated, leading to bladder and kidney problems in later life, if fed too much dry food. Many cats like a drink of milk after a meal, though some may develop diarrhoea if given too much milk. Milk or food should never be fed straight from the fridge, but allowed to come to room temperature first.

Finally, though flesh-eaters, cats need access to grass. It aids their digestion and helps them get rid of accumulated fur in their stomachs. If they do not have access to a garden, then provide them with a pot of grass. The best kind is cocksfoot (*Dactylis glomerata*) and you can buy it in little pots (rather like those in which mustard and cress is sold) from pet shops to grow at home, or obtain it as seed from organizations like the Cats' Protection League.

# MICE BEFORE MILK

Lat take a cat and fostre hym wel with milk
And tendre flessch and make his couche of silk,
And lat hym seen a mouse go by the wal,
Anon he weyvith milk and flessch and al,
And every deyntee that is in that hous,
Suich appetit he hath to ete a mous.

GEOFFREY CHAUCER (1340?–1400)
from 'The Manciple's Tale'
in *The Canterbury Tales*,
written about 1387

This bright-eyed six-year-old is called Sox. He was brought up with a Yorkshire terrier and prefers dogs to other cats. He follows his owner, Mrs Dilys Evans of Hove in Sussex, to the local paper shop and waits outside for her, and very naughtily raids birds' nests, putting the eggs, still warm and uncracked, at his owner's feet.

# FAT CATS

The largest cat in Britain is reputedly Poppa, who lives with his mistress in Gwent, South Wales, and weighs in at an enormous 44lb (20kg). Himmy, an Australian cat, holds the world's heaviest cat title, at the last count in 1982 weighing a gargantuan 45lb 10oz (20.6kg).

But probably the most renowned heavyweight of the feline world was Tiddles, who lived in the ladies' lavatory in London's Paddington station. The tiny Tiddles arrived as a stray when six weeks old. Adopted by the lavatory attendants, he was soon the toast of all who passed through, and as his girth increased, he began to receive fan mail from all over the world. On his outsize, silk-festooned basket, a card proclaimed 'I can walk, run and jump if I want to'. Mostly he sat in lordly disdain. Sadly, Tiddles was put down in November 1983.

Four-and-a-half-year-old Sophi, owned by Richard Thomson of Colne in Lancashire, is very good at opening doors. Unfortunately she has never learned to close them behind her.

# SMALL CATS

There is no recognized 'smallest breed' of cat, although the street cat of Singapore, sometimes called a Singapura, must be a strong contender. As these cats often live in drains, perhaps their lack of size is not surprising. Cases of feline dwarfism account for records of very tiny fully grown cats. The smallest cat ever recorded is a Siamese/Manx cross, resident in Idaho, USA. When four years old, he weighed only 1lb 12oz (790g) although his appetite was that of any normal-sized cat.

# CAT
# CURIOSITIES

There have been a number of recorded examples of freak cats with double tails, extra toes and ears, and so on. The greatest number of toes found on a cat is believed to have occurred on an American cat called Mickey Mouse, who lived in California and had eight toes on each paw.

But one of the most extraordinary curiosities that occur from time to time in the feline world must be the possession of 'wings'. The earliest report of a winged cat was in 1899. The cat, which lived in Somerset, had two fur-covered appendages which came out of its back, and which flapped about as the cat ran. In the 1930s one winged cat was exhibited at Oxford Zoo, and another at a Blackpool museum. There have also been several reported cases of winged cats in North America.

In 1949 a man in Sweden shot and killed one of these cats. It weighed 20lb (9kg), and had a 'wingspan' of 23 inches (58 centimetres).

# CATS AND WRITERS

Throughout history, cats and writers have had a very close relationship. Indeed, the list of writers who have had more than just a passing fondness for cats, who were, in fact, devoted to them, is a long one. Aldous Huxley, it is said, when asked for advice by a young man who wanted to be a writer, replied: 'If you want to write, keep cats.' Whether the young man followed the advice is not known, but many giants of literature certainly did.

The Italian poet Petrarch was so enamoured of his cat that, when he (Petrarch) died, the cat was killed, mummified and buried with him. Other writers did not go to such lengths but Henry James enjoyed writing with a cat perched on his shoulder, and the original macho man, Ernest Hemingway, kept as many as thirty cats at one time and allowed his especial favourites to dine at the table with him.

Baudelaire, Walter de la Mare, Samuel Johnson, the Brontës, John Keats, Alexandre Dumas, Thomas Hardy, Edgar Allan Poe, H.G. Wells, Edward Lear, Rudyard Kipling, Charles Dickens, Mark Twain, Emile Zola, W.B. Yeats, Colette, Mazo de la Roche, Paul Gallico, T.S. Eliot, Dorothy L. Sayers, P.G. Wodehouse and Raymond Chandler are just a few other ailurophilic writers who lived with and wrote about 'the tribe of the tiger'.

# HODGE

I never shall forget the indulgence with which he treated Hodge, his cat; for whom he himself used to go out and buy oysters, lest the servants having that trouble should take a dislike to the poor creature. I am, unluckily, one of those who have an antipathy to a cat, so that I am uneasy when in the room with one; and I own, I frequently suffered a good deal from the presence of the same Hodge. I recollect him one day scrambling up Dr. Johnson's breast, apparently with much satisfaction, while my friend, smiling and half-whistling, rubbed down his back, and pulled him by the tail; and when I observed he was a fine cat, saying, 'Why, yes, Sir, but I have had cats whom I liked better than this'; and then, as if perceiving Hodge to be out of countenance, adding, 'but he is a very fine cat, a very fine cat indeed.'

JAMES BOSWELL (1740–95)
from *Life of Johnson*, 1791

# CATS AND ARTISTS

The languid grace, beautiful shape and colouring and, not least important, ability to stay still, have made cats the ideal companions and subjects for artists for centuries. The American Primitives and French Impressionists, in particular, painted cats time and time again.

Renoir, Bonnard, Picasso, Matisse, Ingres, Douanier Rousseau, Aubrey Beardsley, Theophile Steinlen, Raoul Dufy, Hogarth, Louis Wain, Manet, J.B. Perronneau, Samuel Miller, Tsugouharu Foujita, Gustave Doré, Sir John Tenniel, Arthur Rackham, Felix Vallotton and David Hockney are just a few of the artists who have tried to capture both the spirit and the flesh of this independent creature.

Photographer Francis Loney's blue Burmese, Justin (on the left of the picture) and Jasper (on the right).

# FULL STEAM AHEAD

One of the most bizarre events concerning cats must have been the opening of a cat-racing track at Portisham, near Weymouth in Dorset, in 1936. The course was 220 yards (201 metres) long, and the competitors chased an electric mouse. About fifty cats competed in the races, and the best runners were said to be the two- and three-year-olds. It doesn't sound the kind of event a cat lover would want to be involved in.

A frightened cat has been timed at running 27 miles per hour (43.2 kilometres per hour) – slightly faster than a human sprinter, and considerably slower than a greyhound, which has been timed at 41.72 miles per hour (67.14 kilometres per hour).

# HOME
# SWEET HOME

In the autumn of 1985 Mrs Margaret Evans of Diss in Norfolk was cleaning out the back of her estate car prior to driving fifty miles to RAF Bentwaters. Unbeknown to her, Misty, her four-year-old cat, jumped in the back before she set off and settled down among the blankets there.

When Mrs Evans arrived at her destination Misty leapt out of the car and streaked off into the woods. The family hunted high and low for him but he had well and truly disappeared. They returned to the site the next two weekends and searched everywhere and posted up notices, but there was no trace of Misty.

Two months later Mrs Evans heard a pitiful mewing outside and opened the door to find Misty lying exhausted on the mat. He looked like a bag of bones covered with fur, his eyes were running, his face was torn from pushing through hedges and his paws were very sore. Misty recovered from his ordeal, and the family thought he was very clever – for he made it home in time for Christmas.

One-year-old Don Luigi, winner of the Best Dressed Cat of the Year Award. Don Luigi always looks as if he's stepped straight out of a Savile Row tailor's, but he has brains as well as beauty. He is so adept at opening the fridge that a lock has had to be fitted, and is also inclined to rummage through the kitchen bin. He is keen on ball games, too, and is so pampered that he has two personal sheepskin rugs to sleep on. No wonder he looks so sleek! Don Luigi's owner is Richard Stewart of Cambridge.

# GOOD GROOMING

Although cats keep themselves very clean they do benefit from regular grooming. This helps to remove the loose hair, which otherwise is swallowed and lies in the stomach to form a ball; it means that the owner can examine the cat and keep a look out for signs of injury or parasites; and it is useful for the cat to be accustomed to being handled, in case it ever needs nursing or first aid. It also helps the animal to maintain a clean, glossy coat, and in the case of long-haired cats is essential if a tangled and matted coat is to be avoided.

A soft brush and a metal comb are all that is required; a stiffer brush may be needed to cope with a long-haired cat. Use the brush and comb against the direction of the hair for a long-hair and in the direction of the hair for a short-hair. If there are signs of scurf, then add half a teaspoon of olive oil or corn oil to your cat's food once a day, and it should clear up.

Check the eyes, ears and mouth in the grooming routine. The eyes should not run, but any small amount of moisture or dirt can be wiped from the corners with moist cotton wool. The ears should be clean and free from any smell, and it is not a good idea to poke things into them to clean them. If necessary wipe them with moist cotton wool and dry thoroughly afterwards. If there are signs of a smell or discharge from the ears then take the cat to a vet.

Cats in hard-water areas develop tartar on their teeth in the same way that humans do. It can be chipped off with a thumb nail. If it is left it will make the cat's mouth sore and may mean that its teeth will have to be scaled by the vet, under anaesthetic.

# MY CAT
# JEOFFRY

*For I will consider my cat Jeoffry.*
*For he is the servant of the living God, duly and daily serving
    him.*
*For at the first glance of the glory of God in the East he
    worships in his way.*
*For this is done by wreathing his body seven times round
    with elegant quickness.*
*For when he leaps up to catch the musk, which is the blessing
    of God upon his prayer.*
*For he rolls upon prank to work it in.*
*For having done duty and received blessing he begins to
    consider himself.*
*For this he performs in ten degrees.*
*For first he looks upon his fore-paws to see if they are clean.*
*For secondly he kicks up behind to clear away there.*
*For thirdly he works it upon stretch with the fore-paws
    extended.*
*For fourthly he sharpens his paws by wood.*
*For fifthly he washes himself.*
*For sixthly he rolls upon wash.*

For seventhly he fleas himself, that he may not be interrupted
  upon the beat.
For eighthly he rubs himself against a post.
For ninthly he looks up for his instructions.
For tenthly he goes in quest of food.

CHRISTOPHER SMART (1722–71)
from *Rejoice in the Lamb,
A song from Bedlam*

# THE CATS'
# WHISKERS!

In December 1982 four clever cats called Tango, Tumbleweed, Henry and Bluebeard inspired their owners to invent a board game which, three years later, came to be marketed by Spears under the name Cats' Mansion.

Judith Duffey, art historian, designer and practising textile artist, and Michael Harding, professional astrologer and designer of equipment for the disabled, as well as of games, were preparing for their Christmas holiday when a neighbour's burst pipe put their flat out of action. Martin Davison, a friend who had worked as a games designer for seven years, offered to put them – and their two cats – up in his house for the holiday period. Martin had two cats of his own, who were not pleased at this feline invasion. A subtle strategy game developed as the four manoeuvred for the favoured spots in the house, and it soon became clear to the human observers that the cats' objectives were far from straightforward. A prized cushion would be discarded as soon as it had been won, a place by the fire vacated after much hissing had secured it. No cat was really letting on what it wanted – and this became the basis of the Cats' Mansion game.

The game is played on the floor plan of a large country house with five feline 'men', who use stealth and strategy to find the rightful object of their attention, interspersed with moments of hissing, miaowing and mayhem, where speed of response can

Tabby and white Begel helps Michael Harding (hands, left) and Martin Davison (hands, right) test an early version of Cats' Mansion.

beat the subtlest of manoeuvres provided you know what everyone else is really up to! Bluff and feline cunning abound, and a clever move can turn the game round with the speed of a cat's paw.

Winners in the Feline Personality of the Year Award received Cats' Mansion games, and well over half a million have now been sold. It just shows what an inspiration cats are to their owners!

# PUSSY PLACE-NAMES

Our feline friends have managed to lend their names to a number of places in different parts of the world. There is Catskill and the Catskill Mountains, in America; Cat Island in the Bahamas; even Cape Catastrophe in Southern Australia! But leaving out names like the latter, such as Catterick, Catterline, Catterall and Cattistock, here are some British cat place-names.

**Cat Bells** (Cumbria)
**Catcott** (Somerset)
**Catcleugh Reservoir** (Northumberland)
**Catcliffe** (South Yorkshire)
**Catfield** (Norfolk)
**Catfirth** (Shetlands)
**Catford** (South-East London)
**Catforth** (Lancashire)
**Catlow** (Lancashire)
**Catsfield** (East Sussex)
**Catstone Hill** (Borders)
**Catwick** (Humberside)
**Catworth** (Cambridgeshire)

# UNUSUAL CATS

There are so may different breeds of cats today that it would be virtually impossible to name them all. Moreover, a breed recognized in one country may well not be recognized in another, and breeds change, grow and disappear all the time. There are breeds in existence today which weren't dreamed of ten or even five years ago. There are also new varieties within a breed which have usually come about as a result of careful matings (although sometimes a happy accident has resulted in a new breed).

Here are just a few of the most unusual:

| | |
|---|---|
| **The Sphynx** | A hairless cat from Canada; the only cat to sweat (other than through its paws). |
| **American Peke-faced Persian** | A cat bred to resemble a Pekingese to such an extent that, like the dog, it often has difficulty breathing. |
| **The Rex** | A cat with a very sparse, curly woolly coat. |
| **The Manx** | A cat with no tail, and long rabbit-like hind legs. |
| **The Ragdoll** | A large cat with a long coat and Siamese-type coloured points. An American breed, it is very gentle and has absolutely no conception of danger. Hangs like a limp rag doll when carried. |

| | |
|---|---|
| **Maine Coon** | An American breed which can have fur like a raccoon's coat. |
| **Tonkinese** | The first breed to originate in Canada – a cross between a Siamese and a Burmese. |
| **The Bombay** | Has a shiny black coat like leather – a cross between a Burmese and American short-hair. |
| **Balinese** | Has a long-haired silky coat and huge, plume-like tail. |
| **Odd-eyed White** | A short-hair with one orange eye and one blue eye. |
| **Scottish Fold** | The only breed of cat with drooping ears. |
| **Japanese Bobtail** | Indigenous to Japan, a breed with a pixie-like face, huge ears and a short, kinked tail. |

# POLITICATS

Wilberforce, a large tabby cat, thirteen years old, shares his home, No. 10 Downing Street, with the prime minister. He is an excellent mouser who has served four prime ministers: Mr Heath, Mr Wilson, Mr Callaghan and Mrs Thatcher. He recently starred with Mrs Thatcher in a programme on 10 Downing Street shown on BBC television, and has since received a huge fan mail from all over the world.

Mr Steel and Mr Owen do not share their households with any cats but Mr Kinnock owns two, a tabby and a black.

Cats have proved popular with US presidents. Lincoln and Coolidge were both devoted cat followers but 'Teddy' Roosevelt was probably the most ailurophilic president, owning two cats, Slippers, a cat with extra toes, and Tom Quartz, a very mischievous little cat. Slippers was often the centre of attention at press conferences and official functions, basking in the limelight. J.F. Kennedy also owned a cat called Tom Kitten, looked after by his daughter Caroline and son John. When the cat died, a Washington paper published a eulogistic obituary. The Reagans are also enthusiastic cat lovers, with several in residence at the White House.

# LUXICATS

Many top hotels in London and New York have always had cat residents – once kept as mousers, they now remain because, like mountains, they are there. The Algonquin hotel cat was as much a part of New York literary life as the writers who used to gather there.

Probably the most unusual hotel cat is Kaspar, of London's Savoy hotel. Kaspar is a large, beautiful cat made of wood. Carved by Basil Ionides, Kaspar has lived at the Savoy since 1916. He has led an eventful life; twice kidnapped he has always found his way back to his home. He is a working cat; his function is to sit in as the fourteenth guest at dinner parties of thirteen at the hotel. His table manners are perfect, and he sits quietly on a chair throughout the meal with a table napkin around his neck protecting his coat.

# PAMPERED PUSSIES

Most cat lovers pamper their pets to a certain extent, giving them treats like favourite fish, chicken livers, a comfy bed and special cat toys, though whether the recipients appreciate the latter more than, say, a sheet of newspaper to fight or a piece of string to chase is doubtful. But among the very rich, for whom all things are possible, the pampering can go beyond the bounds of credibility. The proprietor of a top fashion house, who had two pure white kittens which were produced by a jet black mother, gave each its own room in his house, with a proper bed hung with silk and a soft pile carpet. The cats were fed on champagne (presumably among other things) which they reputedly enjoyed, and generally led a life of cushioned ease.

Pretentious Pets, a company which operates from Kensington in London, reports that apart from a request for a pure silver collar, the biggest demand in up-market cat accessories is for unusual catnip toys. Their speciality is real mink bumblebees with real suede wings, which the cats can throw about and chase, and there is apparently a huge demand among Kensington cat-owners for these. Perhaps it is as well that cats can't read, or they'd all want one!

William, a half-Siamese neutered male, who has travelled over 22,000 miles in his fourteen and a half years. He lives in Surrey and accompanies his owners on frequent trips to Derbyshire, and has also travelled to Cornwall, Suffolk, Hampshire and Dorset.

# CATCH AS CATCH CAN

Female cats make the best mousers, and tests have shown that well-fed cats catch more mice than those kept hungry in the mistaken belief that they will then hunt for themselves. The cat that holds the record for the best mouser is a tortoiseshell called Towser who lives at the Glenturret Distillery, near Crieff, Tayside, in Scotland. She catches on average three mice a day, and by the time she was twenty-one, in 1984, had despatched 23,000 mice.

The greatest rat-catcher is believed to be a female tabby, Minnie, who lived at the White City Stadium in London and killed 12,480 rats between 1927 and 1932.

# PERSECUTED CATS

The Ancient Egyptians may have worshipped cats, but because the Romans linked the cat goddess Bast with their goddess Diana, deity of hunting and the moon, cats became identified with Hecate, queen of the witches. In the medieval Christian Church cats were considered pagan beings associated with the devil. People believed that cats slept through the day so they could act as watchmen at night to warn the devil's spirits of the approach of intruders.

Heretics carried out rituals involving cats, and in the fourteenth century the Knights Templar admitted worshipping the devil in the form of a black tom cat. At the end of the fifteenth century Pope Innocent VII ordered the Inquisition to seek out cat-worshippers, and in many European cities horrific ceremonial burnings of cats were carried out.

The idea of a witch having a 'familiar' – a helpmate in animal form, usually a cat – seems to have been more prevalent in Britain than elsewhere, and poor old women who kept a cat, possibly as their only companion, were persecuted and tortured. The Witchcraft Act of 1735 was not repealed in Britain until 1951, and superstitions about cats still persist (see page 142). As far away as Japan, which also used to have its tales of witches and cats, there are statues of the Maneki-neko – a beckoning cat with one paw raised – which is believed to bring good luck.

# TOP TIPS FOR PHOTOGRAPHING CATS

Francis Loney, one of London's top fashion photographers, cat lover and owner of two beautiful blue Burmese, Jasper and Justin, provided these guidelines for successful feline photography:

Being able to take good photographs of your cat starts with basic training when it is still a kitten. You should never tease kittens or cats, or smack them or shout at them, but give them commands in a firm, clear voice. A firm 'No!' is far more effective than any other kind of punishment. If your cats have been trained in this way and trust you, then you will find it a great deal easier to get them to do what you want.

**1.** Photograph them when they are warm and at ease, whether inside or out, though there are generally fewer distractions inside.

**2.** It is often helpful to arrange the photography session for just before a meal, for then they will be eager to please you and less likely to wander off.

**3.** Be ready with a range of distractions beforehand. Cats are very easily bored so it is no use just having their favourite toy to hand. Have a range of toys, if possible, as well as bits of paper to crackle and pieces of string to twitch, and be prepared to make a range of sounds to attract their attention, e.g. hissing or

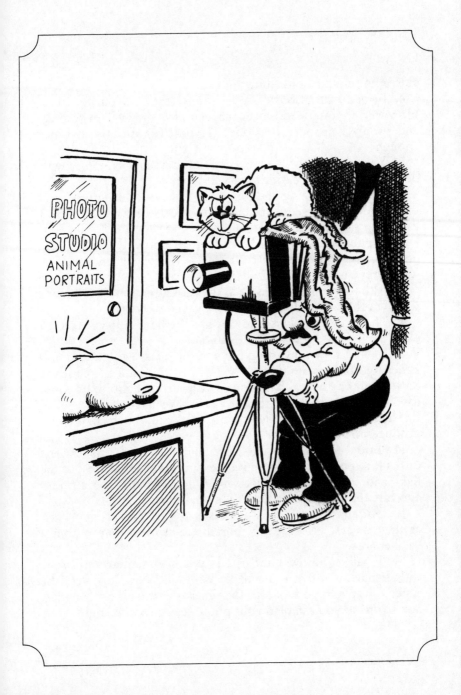

chirruping sounds, or calling their name.

**4.** Bribes can also be used – e.g. their favourite food. However, if you overdo this particular ploy they will get greedy and simply demand more food. A vocal reward is sometimes enough.

**5.** You will need a great deal of patience coupled with determination, so set aside plenty of time.

**6.** If photographing indoors keep backgrounds simple and uncluttered, and make sure that any objects that will appear in the picture pertain to the cat.

**7.** If photographing outdoors there are potentially far more distractions, so be prepared to follow the cat around and see what happens.

**8.** Although you have to keep the cat's attention so it doesn't wander off or go to sleep, don't let it get over-excited.

**9.** The longer the lens you can use the better. If you get up close they will want to sniff the camera.

**10.** You can avoid getting red eyes on a flash-lit photograph either by holding the flash to the side of the camera, or, if the flash is on the camera, by having a very strong light in the room too. This will ensure that the cat's eyes have narrowed to a slit so the light will not be reflected off the retinas, which is what produces the red look.

**11.** Both very dark- and very light-coloured cats can be difficult to photograph, because the dark fur absorbs most of the light and the light fur reflects it. On a dark cat use a wider aperture than usual; on a light cat a smaller one.

**12.** Kittens are in some ways easier to photograph than cats, as they do not get so easily bored and tend to play within a smaller area.

**13.** Finally – know your cat! If you are familiar with your cat's behaviour then you will know its likes and dislikes, the times it wants to go to sleep, the times it is at its most friendly, and so on, so you can plan your photo session accordingly.

# CATS WITH NINE LIVES

Cats are renowned for their curiosity and it is this aspect of their character that has often precipitated them into hair-raising scrapes. There are many tales of amazing brushes with death.

In Ohio, USA, a cat was accidently locked into a brick kiln one weekend. It staggered out the following Monday having endured temperatures of up to 600°F (315°C).

In 1982, a cat called Sedgewick wandered into an electricity sub-station in Cambridgeshire for a little exploration. In nosing around, he received a 33,000 volt shock which caused a power cut in some 40,000 local homes. The badly-singed cat managed to drag himself thirty yards home, where his owner described him as 'looking like a burnt tyre'. After treatment Sedegwick made a full recovery.

Curiosity was not the reason for Patricia's ordeal. This little black and white cat, who was pregnant, was callously thrown off St John's Bridge in Portland, Oregon, USA. She survived the 205-foot (62-metre) drop and then spent several minutes in the icy water before being rescued by some fishermen. She lost the three kittens she was carrying but otherwise made an uneventful recovery and found a new home with one of her rescuers.

Peter, a Dutch cat, survived the capsizing of his ship. Trapped *underwater* in the cabin of the vessel, Peter managed to keep his head in an air pocket while the rest of him was submerged, for eight days, until the ship was brought to the surface. He made a complete recovery.

# KILKENNY CATS

*There once were two cats of Kilkenny*
*Each thought there was one cat too many;*
*So they fought and they fit,*
*And they scratched and they bit,*
*Till, excepting their nails*
*And the tips of their tails,*
*Instead of two cats there weren't any.*

ANON

# CATS IN
# ADVERTISING

Throughout history, the cat has played an important role in magic and mystery. Little surprise, then, that cats still feature strongly in one of today's largest myth factories – advertising.

The commercial cat was born in the mid-nineteenth century when it starred in numerous magazine ads selling anything from stoves to medicines.

Today, the cat, a symbol of richness, sexuality and feline grace, decorates perfumes, lingerie and jewellery ads – luxury items all. It also sells deep-pile carpets, exotic drinks and, of course, its own cat food. In addition, it is a major success in the greetings card business. In the summer of 1986, when this book was being prepared, at least thirty per cent of cards in one of the large stationery chains featured cats. Dogs, on the other hand, apparently have a very poor record in the greetings card market.

# CATS ON THE MOVE

Cats dislike travelling but there are times when they have to be transported from one place to another. Here are a few hints on how to make the occasion as stress-free as possible for both the cat and you.

1. Most cats are best transported in a proper cat-carrying basket with bars for them to see out of. The cardboard kind may not be strong enough. Line the basket with newspaper and a blanket, and get the cat used to being in it for short periods in the house before setting out on a journey. And do make sure he cannot get out of it – some baskets do not have very strong fastenings.

2. If you are travelling in a car, then make sure there is adequate ventilation. If the cat is secure in a basket then it will be safe to open the windows.

3. Some cats will travel calmly sitting on a passenger's lap, but do make sure it cannot get anywhere near the driver. If the cat is travelling loose in the car then the windows must be open only a fraction or the cat may suddenly try to jump through one.

4. If a cat gets very hot travelling in a car in summer, then keep a cloth and a bottle of water handy and wipe the cat's fur with the damp cloth. The water evaporating from its coat will keep it cool.

5. Never leave a cat alone in a car. It will be frightened, and if the windows are closed will quickly get too hot and may suffocate. If the windows are left open it may try to escape.

6. Never, ever, put a cat, whether in a basket or not, in the boot of a car, because of the danger from exhaust fumes.

## Moving house

Moving house is a traumatic event for all the members of the family, and the cat is no exception. Cats hate the disruption of their surroundings as things are packed, and will be nervous and edgy. Try and keep them calm and disturb their routine as little as possible. For the actual day of moving it may be as well to book them into a cattery – perhaps for a couple of nights – so they (and you!) are spared some of the problems.

When you introduce the cat to its new home start it off in one room for a day or two before you let it explore all round. Do not let it out for a couple of weeks until it has become familiar with its surroundings. Then cautiously start letting it into the garden for a short period before a meal, so it has the incentive of hunger to return, and shut it in again when it has been fed. If you follow this routine for another couple of weeks or so, gradually relaxing the rules as time passes, then the cat should settle down and not wish to return to its old home. As with getting a new kitten, plan in advance where its sleeping quarters and feeding bowls will be kept and stick to those places. And the old trick of buttering the paws? Well, this may be less of an old wives' tale than it sounds. It is just possible that if the cat spends its time licking the butter off this activity keeps its mind off the fact that it is in strange surroundings.

## Holidays

Cats do not view holidays with the same pleasure as humans and often go off and hide at the first sign of a suitcase. The ideal way of coping with holidays is to have a kind and reliable person to come in night and morning to feed the cat, let it in and out, and make a bit of a fuss of it, for, contrary to what many people think, cats do like human company and can be very lonely left on their own. Cats in towns should always be shut in at night, and this is especially important when their owners are away as then they may tend to stray further afield.

If such an obliging person cannot be found then you will either have to board the cat out at a cattery or take it with you. This is quite possible if you are renting holiday accommodation, but do check with the owners first. It is as well, unless your cat is extremely well behaved and comes when it is called, to keep it in all the time if you do take it away with you. At any rate only let it out when you are there to keep an eye on it.

If all these alternatives fail and you have to board your cat out at a cattery, make sure it is the best you can find. Visit it first to see under what conditions the cats are kept, and book yours in only if you are quite satisfied. Your local vet may be able to recommend a cattery, or an animal welfare society may help. No reputable cattery will board a cat that does not have an up-to-date inoculation certificate, but despite this precaution cats do sometimes fall ill in catteries, even the best-run kind, so there is always a small element of risk involved.

Cat in a bag . . . and out of it. One of the Brandreth family's well-loved cats, Oscar. The other is Oscar's sister, Neville.

# THE TEN BEST CAT JOKES IN THE WORLD

Why did your cat join the Red Cross?
*It wanted to be a first-aid kit.*

What do you call a cat that has swallowed a duck?
*A duck-filled fatty puss.*

What happened to the cat that swallowed a ball of wool?
*She had mittens.*

JEAN: My cat thinks it's a chicken.
DEAN: *Why don't you take it to the vet?*
JEAN: We need the eggs.

What does a cat use to cross the road?
*A purrdestrian crossing.*

What cat owes money?
*A pussy willow.*

What did the cat who had no money say?
*'I'm paw.'*

What sort of cat has eight arms and loves swimming?
*An octopuss.*

What happened when the cat swallowed a £1 coin?
*There was money in the kitty.*

What do you call a cat that strolls around the jungle wearing jeans and black leather?
*The Pink Panther*

# MOST POPULAR CATS' NAMES

Cats tend to be given more unusual names than dogs, and sorting out the most popular names among the entrants for the Feline Personality of the Year Award was no easy task, as there were so many different names! Among the more unusual were Sieglinda, X-ray, Custard, Will-See (because the family couldn't decide what to call the cat and Dad kept saying 'We'll see'), Mr Jupiter, Stanley Albert, Abracadabra and Chopin. But the most popular name was Tiger or Tigger, or even Tig, followed by Kitty, Whisky, Misty, Sooty, Suki, Sylvester, William or Willum, McCavity and Chloe.

Tabatha, winner of the Prettiest Puss of the Year Award.
Known as Tabby for short, she is owned by Cathie Varley of
Darwen in Lancashire.

# CHOOSING THEIR NAMES

Our old cat has kittens three –
What do you think their names should be?

One is tabby with emerald eyes,
    And a tail that's long and slender,
And into a temper she quickly flies
    If you ever by chance offend her.
        I think we shall call her this –
        I think we shall call her that –
Now, don't you think that Pepperpot
    Is a nice name for a cat?

One is black with a frill of white,
    And her feet are all white fur,
If you stroke her she carries her tail upright
    And quickly begins to purr.
        I think we shall call her this -
        I think we shall call her that -
Now, don't you think that Sootikin
    Is a nice name for a cat?

*One is a tortoiseshell yellow and black,*
*   With plenty of white about him;*
*If you tease him, at once he sets up his back,*
*   He's a quarrelsome one, ne'er doubt him.*
*      I think we shall call him this -*
*      I think we shall call him that -*
*Now, don't you think that Scratchaway*
*   Is a nice name for a cat?*

THOMAS HOOD (1799–1845)

# COM-MEW-TERS' PET

T.S. Eliot would have been interested to hear of the cat with two names which resides at a railway station. In 1985 a limping, poor-looking, half-wild tabby turned up at Witley station, near Guildford in Surrey. It looked around, searching for abandoned bits of food such as crisps, but then wandered off. Gradually it became a regular visitor, and eventually took up residence, with full board and the office armchair thrown in. It keeps the station mouse- and crisp-free and has turned into a sleek and much-loved cat. Regular passengers have volunteered to provide a cat-flap into the station office for it to use, but British Rail regulations do not cover such things.

And the two names? Well, the station is manned by Brian Rose and Michael Atkins, who work different shifts. Brian calls the cat Tibby, and Michael calls it Clare, and apparently the cat is purrfectly happy with the arrangement.

# THE NAMING OF CATS

*The Naming of Cats is a difficult matter,*
*    It isn't just one of your holiday games;*
*You may think at first I'm as mad as a hatter*
*When I tell you, a cat must have THREE DIFFERENT NAMES.*
*First of all, there's the name that the family use daily,*
*    Such as Peter, Augustus, Alonzo or James,*
*Such as Victor or Jonathan, George or Bill Bailey —*
*    All of them sensible everyday names.*
*There are fancier names if you think they sound sweeter,*
*    Some for the gentlemen, some for the dames:*
*Such as Plato, Admetus, Electra, Demeter —*
*    But all of them sensible eveyday names.*
*But I tell you, a cat needs a name that's particular,*
*    A name that's peculiar, and more dignified.*
*Else how can he keep up his tail perpendicular,*
*    Or spread out his whiskers, or cherish his pride?*
*Of names of this kind, I can give you a quorum,*
*    Such as Munkustrap, Quaxo, or Coricopat,*
*Such as Bombalurina, or else Jellylorum —*
*    Names that never belong to more than one cat.*
*But above and beyond there's still one name left over,*
*    And that is the name that you never will guess;*

*The name that no human research can discover —*
*But the cat himself knows, and will never confess.*
*When you notice a cat in profound meditation,*
*The reason, I tell you, is always the same:*
*His mind is engaged in a rapt contemplation*
*Of the thought, of the thought, of the thought of his name:*
*His ineffable effable*
*Effanineffable*
*Deep and inscrutable singular Name.*

T.S. ELIOT
from *Old Possum's*
*Book of Practical Cats*

Twelve-year-old Blackie, owned by J. Kelly of Salford in Lancashire, who presumably has no trouble with cat trays!

# CAT LANGUAGE

Cats convey their feelings in a wide range of vocal and body language. The purr, as everybody knows, is an expression of pleasure, but no one really knows how cats produce the sound nor why they produce it. Most cat-owners will be familiar with a range of other sounds, too. It is only people who are not familiar with cats who think they simply miaow! If you talk to your cat it will respond in a number of ways. The answer to a greeting may be a chirrup or a plaintive miaow, depending on whether it is feeding time; if you play with it it may yowl or grunt; if it is feeling defensive it may growl. Some cats are a lot more vocal than others, and the most vocal of all is the Siamese which can produce a whole range of extraordinary sounds, from a cry like a baby's to a yodel. When angry or frightened, cats hiss and spit, and, as many of us know only too well, when courting they make the most anguished caterwauling noise, usually in the middle of the night!

But cats communicate in other ways, too. If your cat is down the garden and sees you approach it will come towards you with its tail held high and the tip bent over – this is an expression of happiness and confidence. A frightened cat will fluff its tail out to twice the normal size, and if it feels really threatened will make the hair on its whole body stand on end, often arching its back and turning sideways on to whatever is upsetting it to appear larger.

When two cats confront each other, a confident cat will raise its hindquarters, lower its head and bring its ears forward, while staring unblinkingly at its opposite number. A submissive cat will look away and lick itself, as if unsure what to do next. Cats often behave like this when caught in what they seem to feel is an embarrassing situation.

A hunting cat will crouch down and flatten its ears so they cannot be spotted, and move slowly and stealthily until the time has come to lunge forward, when it will move with incredible speed. Some cats bring their prey as offerings to their owners, in much the same way as a mother cat will catch prey for her kittens, and although you may not appreciate this it is difficult to do anything about it for the cat is a predator by instinct.

The treading up and down which many cats peform when on their owner's lap is a throwback to their kittenhood, when they would press their paws round their mother's nipples to stimulate the flow of milk. Some cats carry this behaviour to extremes, and will knead at a coat or a jumper and suck at it too, often dribbling – presumably in anticipation of food to come.

Cats are creatures of habit and expect their owners to be so too. They will be found standing in their feeding place when (or before!) it is feeding time and even if they do not utter a sound the look they will give you will say very plainly, 'Come on! Get on with it, don't keep me waiting!' A cat used to lying in a particular chair may, if that chair is occupied by a visitor, sit and stare at the person to try and make them uncomfortable enough to move. Most amusing, or traumatic, of all, depending on your point of view, a cat will often sit and stare at visitors when it considers it is time for them to go and for the family to retire to bed!

Sylvester, from Lincoln, who in his spare time likes riding ponies.

# CARTOON CATS

Dozens of cats have stalked the pages of newspapers and comics, and have had starring roles in films.

Sometimes they are humanized and walk on two legs, and sometimes they keep their feline characteristics – but they are all wonderfully versatile and their creators enjoy imagining what goes on in their minds. Here are a few of the most famous:

Cicero's Cat
Krazy Cat
Korky the Cat
Felix the Cat
Fritz the Cat
King Cat
Garfield
Tom (of Tom and Jerry)
Heathcliff
mehitabel (of archy and mehitabel)

Felix

Tom

Sylvester

Krazy

Fritz

YOU KNOW IT'S A GOOD CURRY WHEN THE INDIAN RESTAURANT DUSTBINS GO INTO NUCLEAR MELTDOWN

# COSTLY CATS

Compared with their nearest pet rival, the dog, cats are not expensive animals to acquire or keep. A moggie (or even a pedigree cat) may be obtained through a vet or the RSPCA for a nominal fee covering medical expenses. A pedigree cat from a breeder, however, may cost as little as £20 or as much as £100 plus. The cost of looking after a family cat is not extortionate. It may be broken down approximately as follows per annum:

| | |
|---|---:|
| Food: | £110 |
| Litter (if you don't have access to outside): | 67 |
| Vet's bills (injections): | 14 |
| | |
| Total: | £191 |

All cat lovers would agree that less than £200 per year is a very small price to pay for the pleasure that cats give their owners.

Of course there can be extras. Cats have been known who walk around with very expensive plastic knee joints; who have had to undergo expensive operations (often through swallowing unsuitable objects such as Lego, keys, rubber bands) or whose eating fads cost their owners a fortune. But they're worth every penny.

# THE CAT OF CLIFTON STREET

Clifton Street in Roath, Cardiff, is a shopping street. There's a butcher's, a dress shop, a chemist, a pet shop, a building society and various other businesses, and it is here that the large tabby tomcat the locals call J.R. has made his home.

He's lived there for seven years, popping into the butcher's for breakfast, curling up for a doze in the dress shop, calling in the pet shop to see what is going on, and settling down to a saucer of best bitter in the Old Howardians Social Club at the end of the day. On cold winter days J.R. curls up on the bonnet of a panda car that's just come off duty, and sits there while the car is still warm.

The butcher, Mr Addecott, and his wife, who runs the pet shop, take particular care of J.R., coming back to their businesses on a Sunday and over bank holidays to make sure he is fed, but the cat belongs to everyone and no one and enjoys wandering from shop to shop. All the shopkeepers love him, and say the place wouldn't be the same without him. As for J.R., he obviously knows when he is well off.

# A MIRACULOUS ESCAPE

In October 1985 a fifteen-year-old tabby and white cat called Tyger was hit by a train – and lived. She is the pet of David and Carol Thorpe, and their three children Rebecca, Luke and Rachel, of Gee Cross in Cheshire.

When Tyger was found after her accident she had lost most of her tail, one of her back legs was hanging off, a front leg was crushed and part of her face was damaged. Despite these appalling injuries she had managed to drag herself up a railway embankment, along a track and halfway across a railway bridge. From her condition the vets thought the accident might have happened as much as twenty-four hours earlier, and they warned the Thorpes that she might not survive – in fact, they thought she might not get through the night. But survive she did, and now, despite the fact that she has no off-side hind leg, only half an off-side foreleg, and is blind in her right eye, Tyger still catches young rabbits and chases other cats out of her garden. Her owner says she is as adventurous as ever, and she is considered a walking miracle by the local people.

Ginger and white Rogan, who attends church service each Sunday. He also likes going for walks, visiting people for lunch and tea, going on car journeys, and has a great interest in pubs. Rogan is owned by Mrs Jane Bailey of Lyme Regis in Dorset.

# TEN TIPS FOR CARING CAT OWNERS

**1.** *Don't* have a cat unless you are sure you can look after it properly for the whole of its life – which can be for sixteen years or longer.

**2.** *Do* have a pet cat neutered, whichever sex it is, to avoid producing unwanted kittens which people may turn out or destroy.

**3.** If your cat goes out it is a good idea to give it a collar with your address and phone number on, so if it gets lost or involved in an accident you can be notified. *Do* make sure it is a proper cat collar with an elastic insert, or it could hang your cat if it climbs a tree. To discourage your cat from catching birds, a bell can be affixed to the collar.

**4.** To protect your furnishings, provide your cat with a scratching post. One of the best kinds is to wrap an old piece of looped-pile carpet round a piece of wood and fix it to the wall at a height where the cat can reach it when on its hind legs. Or wrap the carpet round the stairs' newel post.

**5.** If you want to deter a cat from playing with a particular object, such as a wooden blind pulley which it may bat against the window, rub the object with a raw onion. You will soon cease to notice the smell but your cat will hate it and leave the object alone.

**6.** When picking up and holding a cat always support its weight underneath its hindquarters as well as holding it round its shoulders. *Never* pick a cat up with an arm under its stomach, it will be extremely uncomfortable.

**7.** A frightened and struggling cat can be restrained by wrapping it in a thick coat or blanket before picking it up. This is to protect you from it!

**8.** If possible provide your cat with a cat-flap so it can go in and out as it pleases. A locking flap is the best kind.

**9.** Despite the above, do shut your cat in at night. It is then far less likely to get involved in a fight, a road accident or be injured or stolen by thoughtless or malicious individuals. Provide it with a litter tray in case it needs one, though most cats who have access to the outdoors in the daytime will manage at night without.

**10.** Aspirin, carbolic preparations, strong disinfectants, DDT and other insecticides, rat and mouse poison, woodworm treatment fluid, slug pellets and certain garden sprays are just some of the everyday products which are poisonous to cats. Do take care never to use these things around your home if you have a cat.

# TRAVELLERS' TALES

There are several well-documented cases of cats travelling long distances to return to their old homes. Some travel fast, and tend not to survive for long afterwards, but others seem to get through the ordeal quite well. A cream, long-haired cat called Sugar seems to hold the record for the longest ever journey. He travelled 1,500 miles (2,400 kilometres) between California and Oklahoma in thirteen months, and he was not trying to find his old home, but trying to find the family who had left him behind, thinking it kinder to leave him in his old home with new owners than to subject him to such a long journey!

A ginger tom called Silky travelled 1,481 miles (2,370 kilometres) across Australia, back to his home after being taken on a touring holiday. The journey took him nine months and he died a week after completing it.

A three-year-old British tabby called McCavity also came to a sad end after travelling back home to Kea, near Truro in Cornwall, from Cumbernauld, near Glasgow – a distance of 500 miles (800 kilometres), which he covered in just three weeks. This meant that he averaged nearly 24 miles (39 kilometres) a day, and the poor animal collapsed and died the day after his arrival home. However, a twelve-year-old tom walked 700 miles (1,120 kilometres) from Johannesburg to Port Elizabeth in South Africa in only ten days – and survived to live for another three years! And the slowest travelling cat on record was a

Siamese called Ching, who escaped on a camping holiday in Wales and travelled back the 125 miles (200 kilometres) to his home in Stow-on-the-Wold, Gloucestershire, taking three years to do so!

The most travelled cat on record is another Siamese, a ship's cat called Princess Truman Tao-Tai, who lived for sixteen years on the merchant ship *Sagamire*. She was never allowed ashore, because of quarantine regulations, and is estimated to have travelled 1,500,000 miles (2,400,000 kilometres) during her lifetime.

In 1922 experiments were carried out on a female cat with kittens. She was placed alone in a sack on six different occasions and taken by car on journeys ranging between one and three miles (1.6 to 4.8 kilometres). At the end of the journeys she was put in a box which could be opened by remote control. Each time she emerged from the box she immediately set off in the direction of home, taking eight hours to cover the one-mile journey, ten hours to cover the two-mile journey and seventy-eight hours to cover the three-mile journey.

However, one of the most extraordinary stories of travel concerns a cat and an Alsatian dog, pets of a French minister and his family who lived in a small village. The minister was moved to another church some 140 miles (225 kilometres) away and, though the cat and dog were great friends, he thought that the cat would be happier staying with the new tenants in the familiar home than she would be if they took her with them. After they had moved house, the dog disappeared, and no amount of searching could find him. But seven weeks later he turned up on the doorstep, accompanied by the cat, whose paws were torn and bleeding but who otherwise was none the worse for her adventure!

Mosey, owned by Miss Joey Walters of Blackheath in London. Mosey says her prayers, begs like a dog, and does Elvis Presley impersonations!

# HEALTH AND SICKNESS

Healthy cats are active and playful, neither fat nor thin, have a glossy coat and bright eyes. The eyes should not run, the ears should be clean and free from discharge or smell, the nose should be cool and moist. The cat's breath should not smell, though cats that have just eaten fish or other strong-smelling food may smell of it for a while. A healthy cat will have a keen – sometimes too keen! – appetite, and will not strain when passing water or motions.

A cat's normal pulse rate varies between 110 and 140 beats per minute. It is taken by holding the cat up on its hind legs and resting the index and middle fingers of one hand over the cat's femoral artery where it crosses the thigh bone on the inside of the thigh, almost in the cat's groin. A low pulse rate, say of 50 beats per minute, or a high one, of 150 or 160 beats per minute, indicates that veterinary attention is needed.

A cat's normal temperature is 101°F (38°C), though if it is nervous or excited it may have a slightly higher temperature. If the temperature goes above 102.5°F (39°C) then a vet should be consulted.

Taking the temperature is a little more difficult than taking the pulse rate. It helps to have an assistant to hold the cat, preferably by taking hold of its shoulders with both hands so it cannot move in any direction. You will need a clinical thermometer, which should be shaken down and lubricated with vaseline or baby oil before you start.

The temperature is taken rectally, and about 1 inch (2.5 cm) of the thermometer is slid through the anus by means of a gentle rotary action, letting it find its own direction. Don't let the cat sit down. The thermometer has to be held in place for one minute before being gently withdrawn and the temperature read.

## Signs of ill health

A sick cat may seem listless, off its food, and have a dull coat. One of the most noticeable signs of ill health is when the third eyelid – the membrane that covers the eye and is usually invisible to an observer – protrudes from the inner corner of the eye to cover part of the eyeball.

If the eyes or nose are running it may mean that the cat has cat flu, in which case it should see a vet as soon as possible. Tell the surgery the symptoms on the telephone, as cat flu is highly infectious and they may not want you to bring the cat into the waiting-room.

Mild diarrhoea may simply indicate that the cat has eaten something it shouldn't. Keep the cat on a light diet of boiled fish or chicken mixed with a little boiled rice. If the diarrhoea is more severe, starve the cat for twenty-four hours and then start it on the light diet. If the diarrhoea persists for more than forty-eight hours then it may be a symptom of more serious disease and a vet should be consulted.

Similarly, vomiting in a cat may simply be the result of eating grass and ridding the stomach of bile and accumulated hairs, of having eaten a meal too quickly, or of having eaten too rich a meal. But if the cat has diarrhoea as well, or if it seems listless and off-colour, and vomits more than once, then this could well be a symptom of disease, and veterinary advice should be sought.

## Nursing a sick cat

Sick cats need rest and sleep in a warm, quiet place where they can be undisturbed. They should not be fussed over, but will appreciate being gently stroked and spoken to in a quiet voice if they are not too ill. They should not be groomed, but will become distressed if their fur or bedding becomes soiled. Keep them clean by wiping round the eyes, nose and mouth, and paws and rear end if necessary, with a warm, damp cloth, using a separate piece for the face.

Many cats, especially the Siamese type, are not good patients and are inclined to give up when ill. They may refuse to eat and drink. If the cat refuses food for more than two days it may be necessary to force-feed it. But first try tempting it with strong-smelling foods such as kippers or meat extract. When cats are suffering from a disease such as cat flu they lose their sense of smell. A cat will not eat food it cannot smell – hence the need for trying out pungent foods.

If it still refuses to eat, and worse, refuses to take any liquid, then ask your vet for a syringe (minus needle) and squirt small amounts of glucose and water, and concentrated meat extract, such as Brand's essence, into the pouch at the side of the cat's mouth, holding its head up and stroking its throat downwards to encourage it to swallow. After a day or two of this regime a cat which has been refusing food may well gain enough strength to want to eat properly again. But keep the diet light. Boiled chicken or fish with all the bones removed, mixed with a little boiled rice, should be fed in small amounts three or four times a day until the cat is considered well again. Don't let it go outside, especially if the weather is cold and wet, until you are quite sure it has fully recovered.

## Dosing a cat

A sick cat may well be prescribed pills by the vet. Dosing a cat is not easy to do on your own, but with a helper is comparatively simple once you know how.

Get the helper to hold the cat firmly round the shoulders, restraining its paws so it cannot claw you. Hold its head up and tilted back, and press on either side of its mouth with your index finger and thumb. This will make the cat open its mouth. Have the pill ready, and as soon as the mouth is open drop it right at the back of the cat's tongue. If you do this correctly it will swallow involuntarily and the operation will be a success! But just to make sure, hold the cat's mouth closed and stroke its throat downwards to encourage it to swallow. Cats which have been dosed before are cunning creatures, quite capable of retaining the pill in the mouth until you have given up and gone away and then spitting it out. It is not usually a good idea to try and put the pill in the cat's food, because most of them will very cleverly eat all the way round it – and leave it.

Jenny, winner of the Most Articulate Cat of the Year Award. According to her owner, Mrs Gail Bower of Sheffield, South Yorkshire, when Jenny wants a drink she says, quite plainly, 'Milk!'

# PET REMEDIES

People in Britain spend a lot of money keeping their pets well-fed and healthy, and there is growing evidence to show that it could be money well spent in terms of the owners' own health. It is claimed that pet-owners have a greater life expectancy than non-pet-owners. Among the elderly recovering from heart attacks, strokes, and so on, it seems that having a pet can aid recovery. A survey at an American university showed that the majority of heart-attack patients who survived were pet-owners.

In 1980, American psychiatrist Dr Boris Levinson helped found the Society for Companion Animal Studies in Britain, to study emotional bonds between humans and animals. The society believes that pets can act as effective counters to mental states such as depression and apathy, to the emotions triggered by bereavement, and even to obesity and hypothermia. Dr Levinson believes that pets especially help people who are out of the mainstream of human society – those who live on their own, particularly the elderly, those who are emotionally disturbed and the mentally retarded.

A practical application of this belief came into being two years ago with the launch of the PAT (Pro-Dogs Active Therapy) scheme in Derbyshire. Selected dogs, which had passed tests on the friendliness of their natures, became registered visitors to homes and hospitals. Now there are 400 dogs in the scheme and it operates in forty-three counties in England and Wales. The Royal College of Nursing gives the scheme enthusiastic support, believing that 'touching and playing with animals helps to care, cure and console'.

# CATS IN CLOVER

Perhaps not surprisingly, but somewhat eccentrically, many people prefer to leave their money to the pets who have given them affection and companionship, rather than to distant relatives or impersonal institutions. Here are some very rich cats indeed:

Charlie Chan, a white alley-cat from Joplin, Missouri, USA, who inherited £131,000 from his owner in 1978.

Sukie, Tessa, Pippa, Ginger and Jemma from Tottenham, North London, inherited £65,000 between them in 1982.

Blackie from Sheffield, South Yorkshire, inherited £20,000 in 1975.

# CONTEMPORARY CAT CONNOISSEURS

Princess Michael of Kent
Beryl Reid
Gemma Jones
Pat Coombes
Sarah Brightman
Sandra Dickinson
Liberace
Barbara Cartland
Sir Roy Strong
Rolf Harris
David Bellamy
Johnny Morris
Andrew Lloyd Webber
Peter Davison
John Craven
Cliff Michelmore
Brian Redhead
Derek Jameson
Martina Navratilova
Sian Phillips

Phil Collins
Brigitte Bardot
Jill Bennett
Michael Williams
Judi Dench
Terry Scott
Victoria Principal
Johnny Briggs
Nanette Newman
Ernie Wise
Maria Aitken
Germaine Greer
Kenny Lynch
Angela Rippon
Nik Kershaw
Jilly Cooper
Libby Purves
Sue Cook
Bobby Moore

# TO A CAT

Stately, kindly, lordly friend
   Condescend
Here to sit by me, and turn
Glorious eyes that smile and burn,
Golden eyes, love's lustrous meed,
On the golden page I read.

All your wondrous wealth of hair
   Dark and fair,
Silken-shaggy, soft and bright
As the clouds and beams of night,
Pays my reverent hand's caress
Back with friendlier gentleness.

Dogs may fawn on all and some
   As they come;
You, a friend of loftier mind,
Answer friends alone in kind.
Just your foot upon my hand
Softly bids it understand.

A. C. SWINBURNE (1837–1909)

Indi, otherwise known as Indiana Jones, winner of the Most Beautiful Eyes of the Year Award. The photograph shows him at three months old, and he is a prize-winning Chinchilla, who won three second prizes at his first cat show. Indi goes for walks on a lead and will eat almost anything, though his favourite treat is toasted cheese. He is owned by Mrs Muriel Lee of Kilmarnock in Ayrshire.

# CATS IN FOLKLORE

As might be expected, countless superstitions surround cats, and countless tales and legends too.

Everyone knows that their luck is in if a black cat crosses their path – at least in English-speaking countries. Elsewhere in the world, black cats are considered to be very unlucky, and black kittens are often drowned at birth. In Italy, in the last twenty years, more than one wedding has been postponed because a black cat crossed the bride's path. The Japanese think tortoiseshell cats are lucky; and white cats are considered lucky in America.

From Indonesia and China to the United States, cats were, and still are, supposed to be able to forecast the weather. Sailors in particular relied on the long-range weather forecasting of the ship's cat. There are numerous tales of accurate feline forecasting, and one cat from the US, Napoleon, had his forecasts published in the local paper, so accurate was he. He indicated imminent rain by lying with his front paws extended and his head placed between them; not once in six years were his forecasts wrong – a better record than our scientific forecasters today.

There is a charming Arabian tale, told about Noah's Ark. The original pair of mice on board had bred so prolifically that the boat was overrun. God had omitted to invent the small cat at this stage in the earth's creation, so Noah caused the lioness to sneeze and a cat appeared from each of her nostrils and took care of the mice for the rest of the voyage.

In Japan, short-tailed cats were considered lucky, while long-tailed cats were thought to be able to assume human form in order to bewitch people.

In Denmark, as recently as the last century, it was not unknown for people to bury live cats at their doorsteps in order to bring good luck, while in Scotland it was believed that throwing a cat in the water would cause a shipwreck!

# EXTRA-SENSORY
# PURRCEPTION?

There are many documented examples of cats apparently displaying extra-sensory perception. One such was the pet cat of an old lady called Lucy Pettigrew, who lived in the East End of London during the Second World War. Lucy became known for her habit of arriving in the air-raid shelter before the sirens sounded. She said that her cat always seemed to know when an air raid was imminent, and would ask for his food early, eat only half of it and then lead the way to the door. He only behaved in this manner just before an air raid.

Another London cat became the only civilian cat to be awarded a medal for bravery. She was a tabby called Faith, who lived in the rectory of St Augustine's Church, near St Paul's Cathedral, during the war. That area of London was badly bombed, and after Faith had given birth to a black and white kitten, christened Panda, she became very restless. She wandered round the house anxiously, but finally seemed to make up her mind, and took Panda from his basket on the top floor of the house and carried him down three flights of stairs to the basement, where she hid him in a recess. Three days later, on 9 September 1940, the house was hit by a bomb and destroyed. The next morning the rector searched through the rubble, calling the cats' names, but with little hope of finding them alive. When he reached the spot where the basement recess had been he heard a faint mewing, and clearing the rubble found Faith, shielding her kitten with her front paws, dusty but unhurt. As a result of her brave action Faith was awarded a special silver medal, which was presented to her in October 1945 by the

Director of the PDSA, with a certificate praising her 'steadfast courage in the Battle of London'. It can be seen in the church, beside a picture of Faith.

But it is not only in wartime London that cats have displayed ESP. On 9 February 1971 the Miller family, who lived in San Fernando Valley, California, were woken at 5.50 a.m. by their cat Josie, who was clawing at the bedclothes. She tried to burrow into the bed, then jumped off it and leaped round the room. She then jumped back and tried to wedge herself between Mr and Mrs Miller. The Millers got up, and, bewildered by Josie's behaviour, let her out of the house, whereupon she ran off at great speed. No sooner had the Millers gone back into their house than they heard the rumblings of an earthquake. Fortunately it was only a slight one, but the tremors continued all day and Josie did not return until the following morning. After that the cat behaved similarly every time an earthquake was about to happen, warning the family of its impending arrival.

And in April 1976 Emma, a Buckinghamshire cat, woke her owners in time to save their children from being overcome by fumes from a faulty gas boiler. The children's room was near the boiler, and their parents were not aware that anything was wrong until Emma came into their room, miaowing and scratching at them, and leading them to the scene of the accident, just in time to save the children's lives.

# THE CAT AND THE RAIN

*Careful observers may foretell the hour*
*(By sure prognostics) when to dread a shower;*
*While rain depends, the pensive cat gives o'er*
*Her frolics, and pursues her tail no more.*

JONATHAN SWIFT (1667–1745)

A formidable array of teeth displayed by Ebony, who is owned by Penny Love of Potter's Bar in Hertfordshire. Perhaps the picture should be captioned *batterie de cuisine*?

# PARASITES

## Fleas

Fleas can turn up even in the best-run households. Any cat can pick up a flea from another cat or from where it has been, but if the fleas are dealt with quickly they will not be able to multiply.

Fleas are small, reddish-brown creatures that can sometimes be seen running through the fur. The signs that a cat has got fleas are when it suddenly jumps up, runs a step or two, then sits down and furiously scratches or bites at its fur. If you examine the fur you may see black specks – these are flea droppings. It is sometimes possible to comb the odd flea out of a cat's coat and catch it, but the best thing to do is to treat the cat with either a special cat flea-powder or a cat flea-spray. These can be obtained either from pet shops or from your vet. Pregnant and nursing cats and small kittens should not be treated with flea powder or sprays.

It is important to get rid of the fleas for, apart from the unpleasantness of having them, they can cause tapeworms in the cat if swallowed. Cat fleas can bite humans, though they will not live on them.

When treating the cat you should also treat its bedding as this can harbour fleas too. Special flea collars can be obtained from pet shops and these will help to keep their wearers flea-free for several months.

## Worms

There are two types of worms that affect cats, roundworms and tapeworms. The latter are the more serious and generally affect adult cats. Their presence can be detected by the cat being ravenously hungry, yet remaining thin, by small segments of the worms being found in the cat's faeces, round its anus or in its bedding (they look like grains of rice and may wriggle about when freshly passed), and by the generally unhealthy appearance of the animal. They are easily treated by tablets or powders obtainable from your vet.

Roundworms tend to affect kittens and young cats, though they can affect older cats too. They look like pieces of cotton and can sometimes be seen in the faeces or vomit of the cat. In a young cat they can produce symptoms of pot belly, coughing, and bad breath. They too can be easily treated by preparations obtainable from your vet.

# STAGE STRUCK!

A stage-struck tabby which wandered into the Redgrave Theatre at Farnham in Surrey has become a resident.

Soon after artistic director Stephen Barry left the theatre to start a directorship at Bath the cat turned up, and the Redgrave's manager Tim Flood wondered if the cat was a reincarnation of Stephen's spirit. (Farnham Castle is reputed to have a ghost, so you never know.)

Staff at the Redgrave were told not to feed the cat, and it was encouraged to return to its home. But it insisted on staying, to become pampered by theatre staff and patrons alike.

It wasn't difficult to find a name for this feline of the footlights. It is, of course, Gus, the theatre cat, after T.S. Eliot's Gus in *Old Possum's Book of Pratical Cats.*

Two pictures of Teddy, winner of the Action Cat of the
Year Award. In the top picture Teddy is playing Subbuteo,
and in the lower one he is watching his favourite television
sport, snooker. When a snooker ball went into a pocket
Teddy would look under the television for it.

Teddy was so called because he was the colour of a teddy
bear. He was owned by the three Taylor children – Maxine,
aged fifteen, Lawrie, aged twelve, and Louis, aged nine, of
Grimsby, who loved him dearly. But poor Teddy came to a
horrible end because he ate rat poison that someone had
put down, and bled to death. Could there be any more
poignant warning against using such chemicals?

# CAT IN A SPIN

In January 1986 five-month-old lilac Persian Harvey's curiosity landed him in a flat spin – literally. For his owner, Mrs Kathleen Bromley of Cowplain in Hampshire, had just put some dirty clothes in the automatic washing machine and gone off to collect the rest of the load when Harvey decided to investigate. When Mrs Bromley returned and put the rest of the washing in the machine she did not notice that Harvey was in among the clothes, and switched it on. She heard miaowing but thought Harvey must have got shut in a room by mistake so went to look for him, and it was several minutes before she discovered that he was in the washing machine. Her husband Peter switched it off and opened the door – and out came a stream of water and Harvey, looking extremely bedraggled but still conscious. He was rushed to the vet and made a complete recovery, though his nose for adventure still gets him into trouble. His owners have to stop him walking on the cooker's hotplate, and generally have to keep a very careful eye on him, for fear of further cat-astrophe!

# BIG BUSINESS

In the UK as a whole we spend £281 million a year on cat food, and £23 million on cat litter (1983 figures). The most popular brands of tinned cat food, which in 1983 accounted for 94 per cent of the proprietary cat food market, are shown below. The figures at the side give that product's percentage share of the total tinned cat food market for that year.

| | % |
|---|---|
| Whiskas | 46 |
| Kattomeat | 10 |
| Kit-e-Kat | 14 |
| Katkins | 7 |
| Felix | 5 |
| Choosy | 3 |
| Supermeat Choosy | 3 |
| Top Cat | 3 |
| Bonus | 2 |
| Nine Lives | 3 |
| House brands/others | 7 |

Interestingly, Whiskas, Kattomeat and Kit-e-Kat were the three foods on which the greatest amount of money was spent in advertising in the same period.

The percentage of tinned cat food bought by different sectors of the population shows that it is more popular in the southern half of the country. The areas are those of the television regions, the figures the percentage of sales for 1983.

|  | % |
|---|---|
| London | 28 |
| Anglia | 7 |
| Southern | 10 |
| Wales and West | 11 |
| Midlands | 14 |
| Lancashire | 13 |
| Yorkshire | 8 |
| Tyne Tees | 3 |
| Scotland | 6 |

Dry cat foods account for only 6 per cent of the total cat food market. The most popular brands, and their percentage shares of the market for 1983, are given below.

|  | % |
|---|---|
| Go-cat | 40 |
| Munchies | 40 |
| Purina Dinners | 9 |
| Meowmix | 8 |
| Loose (various) | 3 |

# POETRY
# IN MOTION

When T.S. Eliot wrote about Skimbleshanks, Bustopher Jones, the Rum Tum Tugger and other feline characters in *Old Possum's Book of Practical Cats,* a poetry book for children published in 1939, he could have had little idea of the success it would have on the stage in the 1980s. By 1986 Andrew Lloyd Webber's musical, *Cats,* had been running in London's West End for five years, during which time it has been sold out for every single performance and has been seen by approximately two and a half million people. In addition to the London production there are ten others being shown round the world – in Australia, Hungary, Germany, Norway, the United States – and two more planned for Paris and Amsterdam in 1987. If you want to book seats for a Saturday night performance in London you will have to wait for six months; for any other night of the week for three to four months. So now you know!

Whiskey, the home-made wine connoisseur. This five-year-old tom is owned by Ted and Susan Hobbs of Bedford. His hobby is collecting small items such as wood screws and Brussels sprouts from the kitchen and carrying them upstairs to stuff into the toes of his owners' slippers in the bedroom.

Demster, owned by Mrs J. Judkins of Cholderton, Wiltshire.
His hobby is climbing among the potted plants, and smiling
sheepishly (or cattishly) when caught.

# CAT-CH PHRASES

Poets and writers have often written lyrically about cats – Kipling, Hardy, Keats and Lewis Carroll, to name but a few, but cats also feature strongly in our everyday conversations. Here are a few well-known aphorisms:

'A cat may look at a king.'
'Curiosity killed the cat.'
'No room to swing a cat.'
'Raining cats and dogs.'
'Cat got your tongue?'
'Playing cat and mouse.'
Looking like 'the cat who got the cream'.
Smiling like 'a Cheshire Cat'.
Having a 'cat-nap'.
'Cat among the pigeons.'
'Cat on hot bricks.'
'Enough to make a cat laugh.'
'See which way the cat jumps.'
'Let the cat out of the bag.'
Looking like 'something the cat brought in'.

# THE TEN WORST CAT JOKES IN THE WORLD

DETECTIVE: I'm on the trail of a cat burglar.
SERGEANT: *How do you know it was a cat burglar?*
DETECTIVE: All it stole was a pint of milk and a saucer.

What did the cat rest its head on when it went to sleep?
*A caterpillar.*

Did you ever see a catfish?
*Yes.*
How did it hold the rod?

What do cats have for elevenses?
*Kit-Kats.*

MRS BIGGLES: Have you put the cat out, dear?
MR BIGGLES: Yes, I've just trodden on its tail.

CUSTOMER: Do you sell cats' meat?
BUTCHER: Only if they're accompanied by a human being, madam.

A black and white cat crossed my path this morning. Since then my luck has been decidedly patchy.

BILLY: I've lost my cat.
MILLY: Why don't you put an advert in the paper?
BILLY: Don't be silly, my cat can't read.

Which pantomime is about a cat in a chemist's shop?
*Puss in Boots.*

JAYNE: I wish I had enough money for a pedigree Siamese cat.
WAYNE: What do you want a Pedigree Siamese cat for?
JAYNE: I don't want one. I just wish I had that much money.

C

C was Papa's gray Cat,
    Who caught a squeaky Mouse;
She pulled him by his twirly tail
All about the house.

EDWARD LEAR (1812–88)

Tarka, taking a rest from doing the decorating. He is a pedigree British Short-hair, aged four, whose real name is Comulus Conqueror, but he is known as Tarka because of his love of water. He is owned by Mr and Mrs Price of Halesowen, West Midlands, whom he wakes in the morning by miaowing loudly, or, if that fails, by leaping on them from the top of the wardrobe!

# A REMARKABLE PHOTOGRAPHER

Harry Whittier Frees was a remarkable animal photographer who lived in Oaks, Pennsylvania, USA, from 1879 to 1953. His work was inspired by an occasion on which a toy bonnet was put on a cat's head, and he went on to take a whole range of photographs of cats (and sometimes of dogs) dressed for the occasion, whether it be going to school, listening to the radio, washing up or going to bed.

In a magazine article published some sixty years ago, Mr Frees said that producing his pictures took lots of patience and practice, and that none of the animals received special training or was forced in any way to produce the poses. Indeed, his star performer, a cat called Rags, was said to hold a pose for several minutes without moving, which is just as well as Mr Frees gave most of his photographs a full second's exposure.

His pictures are reproduced by kind permission of Anne R. Bradford, compiler and publisher of *The Animal Magic of Harry Whittier Frees*, from which the photographs were taken. Ms Bradford had a reproduction of 'All is Vanity' made in porcelain on the headstone erected on Frees's hitherto unmarked grave in Clearwater Cemetery, Florida, in 1979, on the centenary of his birth.

*All is vanity*

SCHOOL — *The little things that count*

Kristy, an eighteen-month-old ginger tabby owned by Mr and Mrs Lucien Roberge of Newmarket in Suffolk. Kristy gets bathed once a week, and came fifth in the Best Groomed Animal class at an amateur pets show – the only cat to be placed.

Kristy wakes Mr Roberge when it is time to get up for work in the morning, but one morning last year woke his owners much earlier than usual by mewing loudly and jumping up and down on the bed. The Roberges got up and Kristy darted from the bedroom into the lounge, where they discovered water dripping from the ceiling. This was even more of a hazard than Kristy knew, for the flat is heated by elements in the ceiling and a very dangerous situation could have arisen. Kristy saved the day!

# IN LOVING MEMORY

Pet cemeteries are full of often elaborate gravestones erected by heartbroken companions for their feline friends. Lettering is often done on marble scrolls, plastic flowers in glass cases abound, and often the graves are decorated with statues of the pet, or of St Francis. Sometimes its toys are scattered there too. In the US such cemeteries are legion and Britain too now has its fair share.

Most inscriptions are simple, merely naming the cat and paying tribute for years of love and affection. Others are more fulsome:

> *No. Heaven will not Heaven be*
> *Unless my cats are there to welcome me.*

Some paraphrase John Greenleaf Whittier's Elegy to his dead cat Bathsheba:

> *Bathsheba: To whom none ever said scat,*
> *No worthier cat*
> *Ever sat on a mat*
> *Or caught a rat:*
> *Requies-cat.*

Here are some of the more humble variety:

> *Mister Podge*
> *Gone to find a sunny spot.*
>
> *Spider*
> *Love and crunchies.*
>
> *Cherie*
> *Our darling little Siamese*
> *Remembered forever with deep love for her beauty and devotion.*
>
> *Requiescat in pace*
> *Scruffy 20–2–86*
> *A special cat*
> *Joe 21–11–85*
> *A softie cat.*

*Sweet little Nounous*
*Gone to the land of Nods*
*With cats and dogs*
*And little mice*
*On 12–7–84.*

*In memory of Scoobi*
*She was born in love*
*Lived in love*
*Died in love*
*And remains in love.*

*Perfect beauty and innocence was my Yo*
*That's why the Lord chose her to go.*
*He picked her out from all the rest*
*Because He knew He loved her best.*

Even the workers are not forgotten:

## *Our Nicky*

*A gentle lady, missed such a lot*
*Dear Nicky, you'll not be forgot.*

J

*1970 to 3–7–84*
*Entronics Ltd, factory cat.*